All Her Ways

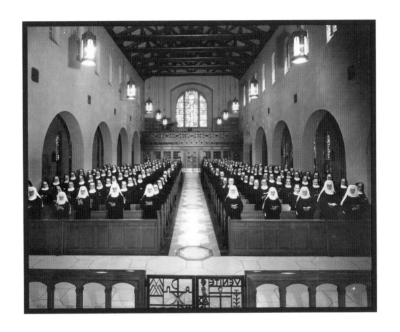

A Short Account of the Foundation, Development, and Artistic Possessions
of The College of St. Scholastica and St. Scholastica Monastery

Agnes Somers, OSB, 1956
Revised and Edited by Joan M. Braun, OSB, 2008

DBB

Duluth Benedictine Books
St. Scholastica Monastery
1001 Kenwood Avenue • Duluth, Minnesota 55811
218-723-6555 • Monastery@DuluthOSB.org

All her ways: a short account of the foundation, development, and artistic possessions of The College of St. Scholastica and St. Scholastica Monastery

Copyright © 1956 & 2008 by St. Scholastica Monastery

All rights reserved. No part of this book may be reproduced or transmitted
in any form by any means without written permission from the publisher.

Text by Agnes Somers, OSB, 1956
Revised and Edited by Joan M. Braun, OSB, 2008
Cover & Interior Design by Tony Dierckins

All images are from The College of St. Scholastica & St. Scholastica Monastery

First Edition, 2008
08 09 10 11 12 • 5 4 3 2 1

Library of Congress Control Number: 2008926535
ISBNs: 0-9815578-0-5 & 978-0-9815578-0-9

Printed in the United States of America by Arrowhead Printing, Superior, Wisconsin.

Published by Duluth Benedictine Books with the help of

Duluth, Minnesota • 218-310-6541

The Benedictine Sisters of St. Scholastica Monastery dedicate this revised edition of All Her Ways *to the Sisters who founded The College of St. Scholastica.*

Stanbrook Hall, the Chapel of Our Lady Queen of Peace, and Tower Hall in the early 1950s when Sister Agnes Somers wrote this book

Contents

Foreword vii

Preface ix

Coat of Arms of The College of St. Scholastica x

Part One: Historical

    I.   Early Educational Foundations of the Benedictine Sisters of Duluth 1

    II. Natural Environment of the College 9

    III. Founding of the College 19

    IV. Standardization 31

    V. To Wider Fields 41

Part Two: Artistic

    VI.   The College Buildings and Their Architecture 57

    VII. Appointments of the Chapel 73

    VIII. Stained Glass Windows 83

    IX.   The Benedictines in the Liturgical Revival 95

    X.   Statuary of the College and Monastery 105

    XI.   Pictures in the College and Monastery 117

Appendices:

    A. Present Locations of Statues and Art Works 137

    B. Descriptions of Building Renovations 139

    C. Donors 140

    D. Architects of Campus Buildings 141

Works Cited 143

Works Consulted 144

Index 145

A 2007 bird's-eye view of St. Scholastica Monastery campus with The College of St. Scholastica when Sister Joan Braun completed this edition

Foreword

This revision of *All Her Ways* began with the need for an index. As the head librarian of The College of St. Scholastica Library for forty-two years, I often wished there were an index for this publication. When people wanted to know about the early days of the College, I would turn to

All Her Ways in its original mimeographed version to try to answer their requests. Often I said, "When I retire and have time, I will create an index for this book." When that time came, the project took on a life of its own, an advisory committee was formed, and this revision has emerged.

I also watched Sister Agnes Somers as she worked on writing this important book. She was going progressively blind but continued to work on her history as best she could. During the summers and holidays, she recruited Sisters home from the missions to type the manuscript, look up information for her, and record her thoughts. At other times when she had no one to help her, she laboriously read her sources with the aid of a magnifying glass, taking notes in her own handwriting. Recording the important events of the early days of the Monastery and College for the benefit of those continuing in the traditions she had helped to shape truly became a labor of love for her.

In the editorial process, the advisory committee decided to retain Sister Agnes' style of writing, even though it might seem out-of-date today. Because she wrote capably in the style of a well-educated student and teacher of the liberal arts in the first half of the Twentieth century, her phrasing and style were retained. We did, however, correct factual errors. Sister Agnes wrote some of this history from memory, since she had been a major force in the development of the College. She is always right in the larger picture of why and how decisions were made, if she is sometimes not as correct in the details. Further, in the style of her time, individuals who had achieved a degree or honor were not named. This convention was true in academia; for example, Sister Agnes refers to herself as "the author." Additionally, individual Sisters did not claim credit for their accomplishments but did their work for the good of the entire Community where all work, from cooking to teaching, was considered equally important. But our modern sensibilities are different; we want to give credit where credit is due and to know who these unnamed people were. Wherever possible, we have named the people she mentioned as, for example, "two Sisters." These changes are made in Editor's notes.

Of course, this edition is not my work alone. Many Sisters, Benedictine Associates, and Development/Public Relations Office staff have assisted over the past five years in bringing this project to fruition. I thank them all.

— Sister Joan Braun, OSB
Editor

Sister Agnes Somers
Prioress of St. Scholastica Monastery
President of The College of St. Scholastica
1924 – 1942

Preface

This small volume is intended for the students and friends of St. Scholastica as a guidebook to the forms of beauty embodied in her history, her environment, her architecture and symbolism, her liturgy and liturgical appointments, her aesthetic possessions—in short, to the many tangible things by which she attempts to justify the claims of her motto: "Her ways are ways of beauty, and all her paths are peace." An exception to the treatment given in the other chapters is made in Chapter IX. Herein the writer has prefaced the outline of liturgical practices at the College with a brief sketch of the influence of the Benedictines in the development of the liturgical revival.

In this book, as the reader will notice, much is made of symbols. A work of art has an inner meaning and spirit; symbols are a kind of language by which that meaning and spirit are expressed. Jacques Maritain, in his *Art and Scholasticism,* says: "The more charged with symbolism a work of art ... the more immense, the richer and higher will be its possibility of joy and beauty." This quotation of an international philosopher suggests that a fuller study of symbols and their meaning would be most rewarding.

More than one hundred art examples are presented in this book. Wherever possible, the name of the artist is given. Two aims dominated the presentation: first, to keep it from being a mere catalog; and second, to eliminate all details that would be in the nature of an artistic appraisal. The explanations given are designed merely to stimulate an interest in the arts by giving some examples of their concrete expression.

— SISTER AGNES SOMERS

Coat of Arms of The College of St. Scholastica

The field is blue; upon this field, a silver lily, blooming with three flowers, rises horizontally, symbolizing the three Persons of the Blessed Trinity. The base of the lily is enclosed by a silver crescent, the heraldic symbol of Mary, the Virgin most pure, and likewise of the purity of Christian teaching. A golden crown of the medieval regal shape in heraldry encircles the lilies above, recalling the dedication of the Chapel to the Queen of Peace.

The heraldic indication of a college is always a book. Hence, a book occupies the center of the field. On its open pages is the motto of The College of St. Scholastica. It is taken from the third chapter of the Book of Proverbs, verse 17, where we read in reference to Wisdom (*Sapientia*): "Her ways are ways of beauty, and all her paths are peace." In keeping with the traditional Benedictine motto, *Pax*, St. Scholastica has chosen the second part of the verse for her motto. It reads in Latin: *Omnes semitae ejus pacificae.*

Part One:

Historical

Mother Scholastica Kerst, St. Scholastica Monastery's first Prioress from 1892-1911

(Previous page: A Sister supervises the planting of a large pine tree at Villa Sancta Scholastica, April 21, 1911.)

I. Early Educational Foundations of the Benedictine Sisters of Duluth

In July 1892, at the invitation of Bishop James McGolrick, Mother Scholastica Kerst and twenty-eight Sisters [THIRTY-ONE IF INCLUDING THREE NON-PROFESSED SISTERS, ED.] came from St. Benedict's Academy, St. Joseph, Minnesota, to open a Benedictine motherhouse and academy

in the recently formed Diocese of Duluth. As the Diocese was new and no home had been prepared for the Sisters, their first problem was to find a residence suitable for their needs. Shortly before their coming, Munger Terrace, a four-story apartment house of many sections, had been erected at the intersection of Mesaba Avenue and Fifth Street, then near the center of the city. Built of buff brick and brown limestone in an English Derivative style, it was an attractive structure, in fact one of the showplaces of Duluth. With these advantages to its credit, it seemed to the Sisters a desirable location for a convent school, so they rented the westernmost section for their convent and the section adjoining it for the academy. At the time, Bishop McGolrick, whose cathedral and home had recently burned down, was temporarily residing at Munger Terrace.

Surely no two persons could have been more generously endowed for a pioneer undertaking in Duluth and its environs than Bishop McGolrick and Mother Scholastica, and their gifts were made to serve not only the many foundations they were to make in the Diocese but the entire population of the district as well. Duluth was then a city of 20,000. Catholics were few; religious bigotry aroused by the A.P.A. movement

[AMERICAN PROTECTIVE ASSOCIATION, AN ANTI-CATHOLIC SOCIETY, ED.] was still rampant, and the prospect of

Bishop James McGolrick, the first Bishop of the Diocese of Duluth (1892–1918)

Munger Terrace was a prestigious address when it was built in the 1890s.

a private school directed by Sisters in what was then one of the most exclusive residences of the city gave it new impetus. Through the influence of the gentle and cultured prelate, the intolerance gradually broke down. In a very few years Bishop McGolrick was an acknowledged leader in Duluth's civic enterprises, and Mother Scholastica's warmth of heart and fine courage had won general approval for her school.

BENEDICTINE SISTERS' ACADEMY AT MUNGER TERRACE

From the beginning, the academic procedures of the little school were strict, and the content of its high school course was strongly cultural. The announcement page of its first catalog reads like the prospectus of an eastern women's college of this time:

> The courses of instruction embrace every useful and ornamental branch suitable for young ladies. At their entrance, the pupils are classified according to their abilities and attainments. A thorough and satisfactory examination is the only passport to a higher department. (*Academic Announcement 1892-93*)

In the program of studies, Religion is given first place. It is a prescribed subject for all Catholics and must be continued throughout the course. Next come the other "useful branches": Rhetoric, English, and

Sister Leonissa Sauber, Sister Pauline Dunphy, Sister Florentine Cannon, and Mother Scholastica Kerst were among the teachers at Munger Terrace in 1893.

American Literature, Mathematics (2 units), History (2 units), Latin (4 units), Chemistry, and Physics. All these are prescribed for all pupils. Some little liberty is allowed in the Modern Languages (French and German), wherein the pupil may select either one after consultation with the Directress. Sixteen units must be earned in the above. The "ornamental branches" include Music, Classroom Art, Sewing, and Delsarte, a system of physical culture designed to give poise and grace of movement. The "ornamental branches" also are prescribed for all but are given no credit.

In the year 1893, as new members entered the sisterhood and the school enrollment increased, it became apparent that larger and more suitable quarters must be

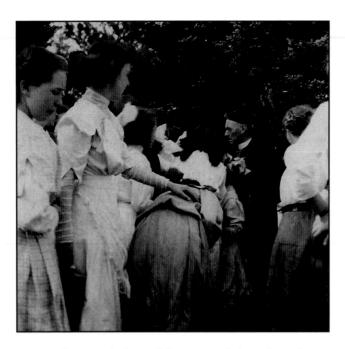

Bishop McGolrick attended a picnic with the students of Sacred Heart Institute in the spring of 1909.

Sacred Heart Institute was blessed by Bishop McGolrick on October 15, 1895, the day before it opened.

found. Not only was the space then available in Munger Terrace quite inadequate, it was not adapted for the purposes of either school or convent. What was acutely needed was a motherhouse and academy planned and owned by the Sisters themselves. Happily, a solution was at hand. Some years previously, Mr. and Mrs. Peter Kerst, parents of Mother Scholastica and Sister Alexia, Mother Scholastica's younger sister and coworker, had purchased lots 55, 56, 57 on Third Avenue East and Third Street, Duluth. These lots were now deeded to the Benedictine Sisters, and the gift was supplemented by a generous donation. At the time, the Sisters were staffing four parish schools and were operating a small hospital in what later became St. Ann's Home for the Aged. With the income derived from these sources forthcoming, and the deed and a goodly sum of money on hand, they were able, in the spring of 1894, to let the contract for a substantial brick structure, the eastern part of which was to serve the Sisters and the western part, the pupils, with space between the two divisions for music rooms, a library, and a chapel

accommodating both groups. The building was to be named Sacred Heart Institute and, according to the specifications of the architect, was to be ready for occupancy the first Monday of September 1895. Eighty-seven boarding and day students registered during the summer months. As it turned out, however, the "Institute" was not completed until October 15, 1895. During the interim the classes were held in a winter chapel of St. Thomas School. Sacred Heart Institute was blessed by Bishop McGolrick on October 15, 1895, and the school opened amid great rejoicing on the following day.

In the summer of 1895 Mother Scholastica sent four Sisters to study at the University of Minnesota in Minneapolis [SISTER JEREMIA CANNON, SISTER AUGUSTINE LEITHNER, SISTER KATHARINE MCCARTHY, AND SISTER CELESTINE SULLIVAN, ED.]. She was probably the first religious superior to adopt such a policy. It was justified, however, since Catholic colleges open to women were then few and far between, and Mother Scholastica, with her strong sense of reality, felt that religious teachers, equally with seculars, should be acquainted with the current trends in education. Her example was later followed in many other religious communities.

SACRED HEART INSTITUTE

Records of the Sacred Heart Institute during its history as a school give evidence of continuous growth. By 1899 the number of pupils had increased to one hundred, and space had again become inadequate. But since brick construction was beyond the means of the Benedictines, a frame addition was built to provide for biology and chemistry laboratories, offices, supply rooms, a store, academic classrooms, and a large assembly hall.

Students and Sisters picking berries at the "Daisy Farm," 1900

Students in a "great tallyho," 1912

An extant school catalog of the year 1900 reveals a curriculum of courses that was solid and sufficiently varied. Religion—including scripture, moral, and dogmatic studies—is basic for all students. In the liberal arts, three programs—the classical, the scientific, and the literary—are listed: the first emphasized Latin; the second, the natural sciences; the third, among other studies, bookkeeping and stenography. In all three programs the graduate must have

earned four units of credit in English and speech and at least two units in each of the following: history, mathematics, a foreign language, and the natural sciences. In the literary program, eighteen to twenty units are required. Music, drawing, needlework, and cooking are general requirements, but no credit is given for them. This is a difficult curriculum in comparison to the high school curricula of the present day!

The next important adventure was a school paper, *The Institute Echoes*, issued for the first time in January 1902. Its aims were announced at the beginning of the editorial page as follows: "The aim of this little paper is to cultivate a literary spirit in the students. It serves also as a bond between the alumnae and their Alma Mater, chronicling the successes of the former and the happenings at the Institute."

The editorial staff of the paper, encouraged by the alumnae and especially by favorable comment in the pages of the *Duluth News Tribune*, adopted a new format, increased the pages from twelve to sixteen, and

The "Daisy Farm" before 1909

included several "cuts" [PICTORIAL ILLUSTRATIONS, ED.] in June 1903. The first nine or ten pages were given over to essays, short stories, poetry, and editorials; the remaining pages to local news, correspondence, a school chronicle, and a comic section entitled "Fact and Fun." The paper, published monthly until 1909, is now a valuable record of the early years of Sacred Heart Institute.

From the first, the administration of the academy insisted upon high standards both in teaching and learning, and education of the heart accompanied education of the mind. Every month the Bishop read the students' report cards and gave a fatherly exhortation on study, sprinkling the long and strenuous performance with

Cutting wheat on the Villa farm in 1913

his inimitable stories. Every week the Directress of the school devoted an hour to character formation and social grace. The school day extended over six and one-half hours, but as this was in accordance with the general practice, no one considered it excessive. Sacred Heart Institute grew rapidly both in numbers and prestige. Its graduates were admitted to state universities and advanced normal schools without examination. It was universally praised for the sound training exhibited by its students. Yet these assets, valuable as they were for a school, did not satisfy the ardent spirit of Mother Scholastica. With an insight that seems to us now providential, she envisaged a larger foundation at some distance from the rapidly growing city, and a situation

Sacred Heart Institute students visit "The Daisy Farm," 1906.

where water, woods, and hills might inspire to ideals of beauty and peace.

Fortunately, in 1900 a site was found that seemed to answer all the requirements. It was an eighty-acre tract, three miles distant from the city limits, and was then called the "Daisy Farm" because of its kindly harboring of the wild ox-eye flowers. From the date of its purchase, the place became a picnic ground for the school population at Sacred Heart Institute. Every spring and autumn, books were forgotten while faculty and students mounted the great tallyhos [FOUR-IN-HAND COACHES, ED.] and set out for a day of perfect enjoyment at the "Daisy Farm." Sometimes Mother Scholastica gladdened the day with her presence. On rare afternoons Bishop McGolrick came too, delighting the gathering with his charming anecdotes and his profuse knowledge of plant and animal forms.

These outing days were red-letter occasions in the calendar of the year, and two of them were truly prophetic. On the first occasion, a party of Sisters and students were escorting their Bishop to the scene of the selected picnic ground, the pine grove. On reaching a level between the hills, the party rested for a moment, and Bishop McGolrick, commenting on the beauty of the vista, remarked: "This would be an ideal site for your new academy: it is sequestered from the public road; its elevation is high; and it commands a splendid view of Lake Superior." Thereupon the members of the party, assenting to his thought, marked the proposed site with a small pile of stones.

Mother Scholastica Kerst and Sacred Heart Institute students enjoy a picnic on Villa Day, 1910.

and its activities are in large measure a realization of the dream of its noble foundress.

At the close of the school year 1909 the *Institute Echoes* suspended publication to be succeeded by the *Villa Scholastica Quarterly*. During the seven years in which the *Echoes* served as the news organ of Sacred Heart Institute, it grew from a twelve-page pamphlet to a magazine of sixty pages. The final issue, published June 12, 1909, was announced as the "Commencement Number." It contains, among other things, two es-

On the second occasion, Mother Scholastica voiced in these words her hope, which has now become a reality: "My dream is that some day there will rise upon these grounds fine buildings like the great Benedictine abbeys of Europe. They will be built of stone; and within their walls higher education will flourish, the Divine Office will be said, and the beautiful ceremonies of the liturgy will be carried out."

Both hopes were to see fulfillment. On the very spot marked by the pile of stones, ground was broken in 1908 for the first unit of the new school. The present College

says, interestingly and correctly written; a really good editorial; a travelogue of several pages from an alumna touring Europe; a page of excerpts from the Bishop's Address at the Commencement Exercises; records of the class play, *The Merchant of Venice*, whose "male roles were so ably interpreted by the girls"; lists of premiums and promotions; cuts of "young ladies picnicking at the Daisy Farm"; records of musical recitals; and a day-to-day chronicle for May and June, written in a sprightly style. Judging by this number, the *Echoes* had lived up to the aims expressed in the first issue.

II. Natural Environment of the College

When in 1899 Mother Scholastica commissioned a land agent to find an attractive site for a new academy high among the hills of Duluth, she voiced a tradition that has been cherished by Benedictines throughout the centuries. A well-known proverb says: "Bernard likes the valleys,

Benedict the hills." Ever since their great founder built the cradle of the Order on scenic Monte Cassino in present-day Italy, the Benedictines have by preference placed their foundations on high sites with beautiful surroundings. And Mother Scholastica found no obstacle to following this custom in the topography of Duluth. Extending a length of twenty-six miles, with an inland lake on one side and a continuous incline on the other, Duluth was destined to become "a city upon a hill." At the same time, it was endowed with many gifts of rare natural beauty.

One of these is an interesting geological formation. Studies of the region show that it is underlain by an intrusive rock of pre-Cambrian age, locally known as

Duluth gabbro forms the base of the Sacred Heart Shrine.

"It is a good and pleasant site . . . with waters, . . . woods, and pleasant fields."

Duluth gabbro. This igneous rock rises to an immense crescent along the side of the lake, running from a westerly to a northeasterly direction. It is soil-covered for the most part, but occasionally outcrops appear in the form of bare cliffs or great boulders, which show that it has been intruded by colorful granites and other stones deposited by the glacial drifts. The lake, formed in a syncline of the gabbro, seems to have originated in the period of glaciations by repeated ice flows from the north. [RECENT GEOLOGICAL THEORIES SUGGEST ALTERNATIVE INTERPRETATIONS. ED.] As the ice retreated, it filled the immense basin, developed an unusually interesting shoreline, and covered the district with rich deposits of sediment. In general, the numerous streams that now drain both the slopes and uplands lie near the surface, since the hardness of the basic stone and the late development of the lake have prevented much erosion. However, the water has in some places cut down to bedrock, forming gorges, which add to the beauty of the landscape.

As might be expected, these factors have all contributed to make Duluth a city of varying heights. The lake is 602 feet above sea level. From its waterfront the hillside slopes slowly upward at first, then steepens perceptibly for a distance of two miles to reach an irregular plateau with an elevation of five to six hundred feet above the lake. The upland is gently rolling with relatively large areas of level land broken at intervals by hills of greater or lesser height. Within these plains, at a distance of two or three miles from the heart of the city, was found what seemed to be the ideal site for the new academy.

Newman, in his classic work, *The Idea of a University*, quotes from a discourse once given by Anthony á Wood in which the old philosopher lays down certain natural advantages that should exist in the environment of a university. Since the charms he requires are those which should be found in the location of a college, we shall recount them and try to discover

"Winter brings much snow, but that means . . . scenes of winter loveliness."

whether they exist in the environs of St. Scholastica. "A good and pleasant site where there is a temperate and wholesome constitution of the air; composed with waters, springs or wells, woods, and pleasant fields; which being obtained, those commodities are enough to invite students to stay and abide there."

First "a temperate and wholesome constitution of the air": Facts and figures drawn from official reports on the climate of the region show that its high altitude and fine drainage make Duluth one of the most healthful cities in America. An Easterner or Southerner who has not lived in this climate would be hard to convince of this. He is likely to have thought of it as the coldest city in America. Tell him you are from Duluth, and he will exclaim with an affected shiver: "What! That cold place!" E. Dudley Parsons, an authority on the early history of the state, believes that the legend of Minnesota's cold originated in the exaggerated tales of explorers or early settlers who boasted of rivers frozen in September and roads blocked with snow in October. As a matter of fact, the weather reports of Duluth over a period of years testify that the mean temperature for its three

A painting by Sister Salome Blais depicts the Chapel in autumn, "nowhere so beautiful as in Duluth."

coldest months is 11.7 degrees. When there is a spell of low temperatures, its duration is only a few days and is due to a general cold wave. Very destructive storms and cyclones do not occur. Winter brings much snow, but that means the conservation of moisture for spring needs as well as winter sports and scenes of winter loveliness. Spring comes suddenly, generally bringing a mild April, followed by a damp and chilly May. Summer, beginning in mid-June, is a delightful season, with temperatures in the comfortable seventies. When a few days of excessive heat happen along in mid-July, they are compensated by nights so cool that one can sleep under a blanket.

No wonder that the grass and trees retain their deep green until the late September frost! The ideal season, however, is autumn—no mere episode in the changing year, but a time of slow transition. After the equinoctial storms at the end of September comes Indian summer, nowhere so beautiful as in Duluth. For the greater part of October the temperature is in the sixties, trees and shrubs wear their flamboyant dress, and the atmosphere is amber-colored. In all seasons, the lake tempers the climate, and, happily, it does so without increasing the precipitation to any significant degree, as comparable figures for regions distant from the lake show.

THE CAMPUS

In the year 1900 the Sisters of St. Benedict selected a site for their academy, later to become a college, on the uplands of the city. The first forty acres of land, purchased in 1900, was doubled in extent by a second purchase made two years later. In 1908 the property was again doubled, making the 160 acres that constitute the present campus. The College buildings are at the very center of the tract, on a gradual slope facing the east and at an elevation of 680 feet above the lake. Rising from this height, they look out upon a panorama of undulating hills, wooded valleys, and clear waters. Fairview Heights, the most prominent of the hills, faces the College at the east. Its altitude of 1,481 feet above sea level makes it the second highest elevation in the region. At its south slope, the College overlooks scenic Chester Park; east of it is a large residential section of the city, where many students of St. Scholastica have their homes. In 1935 the Sisters

petitioned the city government to have a road built over the "Heights." Their request was graciously received, and in 1937 the new road was officially given the name "College Street." Today it is a much-traveled road and is contributing to the development of what promises to be a very attractive suburb of Duluth.

Lake Superior, south of the campus, was named by the Jesuit explorers, who wrote in their *Relations of 1660*: "This lake we call Superior because of its position above the lake of the Hurons" (Thwaites). It has, however, another title to that name. Its area of 32,000 square miles makes it the largest body of fresh water in the world. The lakeshore is not visible from the College, but the immense width of the waters causes them to create what appears to be a new shoreline along the top of the escarpment, where they come forward in a series of charming inlets between the hills. Although three miles distant, the lake gives the impression of being at the very

The City of Duluth built College Street over Fairview Heights in 1935-1937.

The Villa has "waters that flow in smoother numbers" in Chester Creek and its dam.

border of the campus. From there it stretches back to the distant skyline, its waters—noted for their clarity—reflecting the blue above them. In favorable weather conditions, this vast expanse of lake is a most exhilarating sight. Seen in the half-light of a summer evening or in the early morning when the rising sun scintillates upon its surface, it is unforgettably beautiful.

For those who prefer "waters that flow in smoother numbers," St. Scholastica has her own stream, Chester Creek. Entering the campus at the north border, it runs diagonally across the fields to about one hundred yards northeast of the buildings. At this point, the water has been dammed back into a small lagoon that empties over an artificial waterfall of five feet. From there it follows its course across the east end of the campus until it reaches the main driveway, then turns abruptly east and, passing below the street, disappears in the gorge of Chester Park. All along this course, the banks are wooded with willow, cherry, and white birch.

One of the tributaries of Chester Creek, flowing from northwest to southwest at the opposite end of the property, enters a prolonged ravine that cuts through the campus at its southwest corner. The depression of the ravine is so deep and so densely grown with vegetation that the murmur of the stream is quite inaudible from the upland. The first students at the College were greatly attracted by the solitariness of this spot and named it "The Valley of Silence."

"Woods and pleasant fields": This row of trees contains some of the many trees native to the area and those planted to beautify the property.

"Woods and pleasant fields" are certainly not wanting. Besides the plenteous growths that clothe its valleys, the campus has three natural groves. A ten-acre stand of white spruce, interspersed with other conifers, occupies the northwest section. Locally this is known as "the Pines." A five-acre grove of deciduous trees (mostly elm, maple, and cherry) rises farther west. At the southwest is Maryglade, a natural park of thirty-five acres. The area is wooded for the most part, but is diversified by rock formations that appear at the surface of the soil and by grassy glades scattered here and there throughout the trees. One of these open spaces contains a recreational lodge; another, a shrine of Our Lady—the two together accounting for the name "Maryglade," by which the park is known. Students of geology find interest in studying the rock exposures, which show intrusive contacts with the blue and red granite above the gabbro, and in examining the morainic character of the soil. In the days when botany was more popular than it is now, Maryglade was a "happy hunting ground" for students of taxonomy.

Today its chief attraction to the botanist is its tree life. Besides the poplar and paper birch, which are plentiful along the ridges of the "Valley," oak, elm, maple, linden, ash, and other species and varieties (twenty-one in all) thrive in the soil. Several years ago the College planted some hundreds of pines and spruces among the other

A recreational lodge situated among the trees in Maryglade

trees; these have had a sturdy growth once they obtained a foothold.

There are in all fifty-seven species and varieties of trees on the campus. They comprise the trees and tall shrubs native to this northern climate along with a goodly number of others that have been introduced and acclimated by cultivation. In general, the College has favored evergreens for planting because of their round-the-year foliage. In the early years of her history, it was customary at the College for the graduating seniors to plant an evergreen on their Class-day as a symbol of their enduring loyalty to their Alma Mater. It was a significant custom, which incidentally added several new species.

"Pleasant fields" are still to be accounted for. They are not wanting. Between the outlying areas of native wood and stream lies the main campus. In 1926 this was blueprinted by a landscape architect, and about one-sixth of the acreage was assigned to formal lawns and gardens. The plan has been continuously developed through the construction of terraces and concrete walks and the planting of trees, shrubbery, and flowers. Throughout the years this formal treatment has created a place of ever-changing contrast: in winter, its wide stretches of unspotted snow are relieved by the sturdy evergreen; in spring, the tender green of birch and willow forms a background for lilac and cherry blossoms; in summer, lawns of emerald are rich

Maryglade provides "woods and pleasant fields" for the College.

The main (southeast) entrance of Villa Sancta Scholastica before 1921

with blooming flowers, nowhere so intense in color as in this northern clime; in autumn, scattered oaks, elms, and maples are clothed with reds and purples by the early frosts.

In his essay on the Benedictines, to whom he assigns the role of poetry in the arts of civilization, Newman glorifies the Order for its love of natural beauty ("The Mission" 397). It can be said that in her humble way this Benedictine college has continued the tradition. When the gymnasium was erected in 1921, the grounds between it and the former building were immediately improved. When Tower Hall was planned, the acreage was landscaped, and improvement on the eastern confrontation was begun. Grading was pushed forward, sidewalks laid down, and grass was coaxed into a verdant carpet for the terraces and the mall. When this was finished, the land converging toward the gymnasium from northwest and southwest was changed rapidly into an athletic layout with two tennis courts, a small golf course, a baseball ground, a skating rink, and a field hockey pitch. In the spring of 1929 trees, shrubs, and flowers were planted in abundance, and very soon the College had an immediate environment that even old Anthony á Wood might describe as "a good and pleasant place inviting students to stay and abide there."

This statue of St. Scholastica stood near the entrance to the original Villa for many years.

III. Founding of the College

A few days before the opening of school in September 1909, while the Villa yardman familiarly known as Mike was erecting at the entrance from the highway a sign bearing the name of the institution, a passing pedestrian stopped to spell out the words, "V-i-l-l-a S-c-h-o-l-a-s-t-i-c-a"

and asked, "What does that mean?" Mike raised his head importantly and, pointing to the sign with a forefinger, explained, "That means the Valley of Education."

Now, though Villa Scholastica is actually "seated upon a hill," not in a valley, Mike's answer had a certain relevance; from that day to this, education has been the chief concern of the Villa and its occupants, and that not only on the secondary but also on the higher level.

Two years had barely elapsed when, in the autumn of 1911, some members of the faculty came out with the pronouncement that it was now the acceptable time to open a junior college. After the devastating surprise occasioned by this bombshell had

Villa Sancta Scholastica in the era when it became a junior college

subsided and the problem had been argued from every angle, pro and con, the opposing sides were asked to put their arguments in Thomistic form and present them to the Mother Superior [SISTER ALEXIA KERST, ED.] and her Council, who, in the last analysis, would decide the matter. This was done, and the question, "On the Opening of a College," was stated in four Articles, namely: Whether we need a college at this time? Whether we could staff a college? Whether we could get students for it? Whether we could stand the expense?

When the Venerable Arbiters had estimated the values of the different arguments given in the Objections and Replies and had added up the totals on each side, they found a

Villa Sancta Scholastica students in study hall in 1913 (top)
and in an undated photo (bottom)

History, Mathematics, the Natural Sciences, Ancient and Modern Languages, and the Fine Arts.

No doubt, this long array of courses looked formidable to the two girls and four Sisters who presented themselves for matriculation on September 10, 1912, the day on which the College formally opened. But the teachers were happy with six students for a beginning, and, small as the classes were, they prepared their work as carefully as if it were intended for a crowded lecture hall. The students, on their side, made a like return. Not only were they brainy; they worked hard. As one of them afterwards remarked, "Study was our major sport." To the serious purpose and splendid work established at the College by this and succeeding small classes of girls and young Sisters, St. Scholastica attributes much of its success.

Social and recreational opportunities, as compared with those of today, were almost negligible. True, the social hall was spacious, providing ample room for dancing and parties—generally sponsored by the "academics." [THE HIGH SCHOOL STUDENTS OF VILLA SANCTA SCHOLASTICA ACADEMY, ED.] Weekend permits, proms, dinner dances, and the like were still several years in the future. Out-of-door exercise was a rigid requirement. Classes were dismissed at three o'clock, and the girls were scheduled to exercise an hour in the open air before dinner. For the warm season, croquet was provided and tennis on an improvised court; for the winter season, tobogganing and skating on "the pond," a tiny lagoon on the campus, dammed back from Chester Creek. In the summer weather, the girls obeyed the regulation with alacrity.

Besides the formal games there were excursions to the woods—so colorful in spring and autumn—and in the latter season, an occasional descent upon the kitchen garden, where a kind-hearted gardener could be cajoled into handing out juicy turnips, pared with his pocketknife. In sub-zero weather the collegiates evaded the requirement when they could. It seems certain, however, that even then the out-of-doors rule was rigidly enforced.

balance in favor of the College. So the two main proponents of the plan [SISTER AGNES SOMERS AND SISTER KATHARINE MCCARTHY, ED.] were set to work examining catalogs, making out requirements for admission, outlining sequences and credit hours, and deciding on the various minutiae that go into the Announcement of a college.

In view of the mounting cost of printing, no catalog was published that year; but the spring issue of the *Villa Quarterly* gave all the necessary information on the new junior college and listed fifty-two freshman and sophomore courses in eight departments, namely: Religion, Philosophy, English,

One of the students of 1913-1914, now a grandmother, tells how its enforcement paid off. She writes:

> That winter five of us girls obtained permission to study from 3:30 to 6:00 and spend an hour skating in the evening. When the prescribed hour became an hour and a half, then almost two hours, the prefect thought it time to investigate. She discovered that five young men from the city had learned the whereabouts of the pond and were coming out to share our exercise. Fortunately they were found to be "young gentlemen of good families"; hence our permission, though limited as to time, was not revoked. There is no record of Cupid being a skater, but he must be, for three of us made contact with our future life partners during these very exercises.

Perhaps this explains why the administration in preparing the next year's catalog could say, "The advantage of outdoor exercise (on the Villa campus) leaves nothing to be desired."

The same catalog shows how simple, yet stringent, was college life forty years ago. On page 8, under

Villa students enjoyed skating on Chester Creek pond in the winter.

"General Remarks," is this: "The scholastic year is divided into two sessions of twenty weeks each." On page 9, under "General Regulations": "The Christmas and Easter vacations are intended to prevent any unnecessary excuse for a leave of absence. All such absences and extra visits home will debar the pupils from receiving medals, premiums, etc." Again, under the same caption: "Newspapers sent from home are not delivered, as magazines and periodicals suitable for

"The Villa" after 1921 when the gymnasium was built

young ladies are furnished by the Institution." A paragraph on travel connections informs visitors from a distance that, "The street-car line on Ninth Street at Eighth Avenue East is one mile distant from the College. Those who desire it may secure carriage service at a small cost by communicating with the Institute of the Sacred Heart, corner of Third Avenue and Third Street."

This Reception Room was also the Admissions Office.

college work "for Sisters only"; and two Sisters who had been in residence at Catholic University received higher degrees: one, the doctor's, [Sister Katharine McCarthy, Ed.] the other, the master's degree [Sister Agnes Somers, Ed.].

The Accreditation Problem

In September 1914 the enrollment increased to eighteen:

The year 1913–1914 was important to the College in many ways. A stone structure containing classrooms and a one-story garage was built to replace the wooden ramp that had previously connected the main building with the science hall; the plot of ground before the south entrance was laid out as a triangle, with transplanted trees and a statue of St. Scholastica; the outline of courses in the current catalog was extended to include senior

seven Sisters and eleven lay students. As four of the latter intended to go on to a university at the end of the second year and their credits would have to be transferred, the question of accreditation became a major headache for the administration. It should here be explained that in acquiring state approval, there exists always in beginning colleges a situation that is paradoxical; on the one hand, the State University is slow to approve a college

Villa Sancta Scholastica, including the Gymnasium as seen from the back after 1921

with a very small enrollment; on the other hand, most high school graduates are reluctant to enter a college that has not been accredited by its State University, fearing that their credit will not be accepted when transferred. From the time of its opening, St. Scholastica had been striving by constant recruitment and by other means to increase its enrollment. Sisters went throughout the city and the Diocese searching for stray aspirants after a liberal arts education. Each new registrant was looked upon as a gift from God. And perhaps she was; certainly, the faculty kept imploring heaven for the "goodly increase." Fortunately, in the spring of 1914 Minnesota sent an examiner

St. Scholastica students in the chapel in Tower Hall sometime in the mid 1920s

The Art Room in the early College

them at the University must have made an excellent record, since the College catalog of 1916 was able to announce on its cover: "College of St. Scholastica, affiliated with Catholic University, Washington, D.C." Below this was the more modest announcement: "Junior College accredited to the University of Minnesota."

The enlistment of youth into military service in 1917 caused a teacher shortage in Minnesota, and the State Department of Education proposed that St. Scholastica open a normal department for the training of county schoolteachers. Agreeing to this proposal, the Villa added the required

who later reported that approval would be given the College for the freshman year. In 1915 when the examination was repeated, tentative approval was granted for the second year. That fall the first lay student who had attended the College for two years and then transferred to the University of Michigan in Ann Arbor, Michigan, was given a year and a half of advanced standing beyond the freshman year.

In September 1915 two Sisters were given advanced standing for their senior college work at Catholic University. They and the four other Sisters who preceded

courses and engaged as head of the program a teacher recommended by the State. This young woman later entered the Sisterhood [THERESA GLEASON, LATER SISTER BASIL, ED.]. Asked today, she recalls the experience thus: "Ten or twelve students took the courses offered in Methods, Practice Teaching, and Child Psychology while continuing some of their college work. At the conclusion of the program, they passed the County Examinations and secured positions in rural schools. When the war ended and the country returned to normalcy, the program was dropped."

Some Gratifying Results

It seems certain that the College, despite its limited numbers, accomplished much for Christian education in the period between September 1912 and June 1924. Within those years 160 students completed two years of college work at St. Scholastica. Of these, 116 were lay students; forty-four were Sisters. Thirty-four of the 116 lay students continued to the degree level at other colleges or at universities. Of the remainder, some took the county teachers' examinations and taught school, while others worked at other jobs or married soon after finishing the two years.

In the answers to a questionnaire sent on August 25, 1942, to the thirty-four lay students who transferred to universities or standard colleges between 1912 and 1924, all the respondents stated that the credits earned at St. Scholastica were accepted without qualification. Not only did these girls "make good"; two of them completed their work in a year and a half at the University of Michigan; one was similarly fortunate at Berkeley, California. Of the others who transferred to the Universities of Minnesota, Michigan, California; Loyola in Chicago; and to the Colleges of St. Catherine, St. Paul, Minnesota; St. Mary's of the Woods in Terre Haute, Indiana, and San Diego, California, all but two received the coveted degree in two years.

However, the picture is not perfect. One student had to repeat in summer school a course taken in her senior year at the University of Minnesota; a student who entered the Medical School at Loyola University, Chicago, says she "should have had more work in chemistry in junior college"; one who went to Berkeley for her senior college thinks her courses at St. Scholastica were "too booky," having "too little bearing on the needs of practical life." In every other case, however, the answers are in line with those of a lay student who transferred to the University of Minnesota in 1918. She reports as follows: "All my credits were accepted. There were no handicaps. The work at St. Scholastica was a great help to me. If possible, one should take four years at your college and later take graduate work at a large university."

Practically all the forty-four Sisters continued to the bachelor's, many to the master's, and several to the doctor's degree. After finishing two, three, or four years at the College, they transferred to Catholic University, to Minnesota, to Chicago, or to other large institutions. Five were admitted without deficiencies to the graduate school of Catholic University, one to the graduate school of Minnesota, and one to the graduate school of Chicago. Two others were given a year of advanced standing at the latter university. All of the others obtained the bachelor's degree in two years or less time.

First Two Bishops Of Duluth

The College suffered a severe loss on January 23, 1918, when Bishop James McGolrick, Honorary President of

Bishop John T. McNicholas, OP,
second Bishop of the Diocese of Duluth, (1918–1926)

the College, passed away. As first Bishop of Duluth and cofounder of its religious institutions, his passing was a poignant sorrow to the Sisters. By the students, he was regarded as a great leader. One who attended the College in the early years of its development expresses the general regard of the girls in these words:

> Bishop McGolrick was much revered throughout the Diocese and in all its schools. He used to visit our college classes occasionally, attend our picnic each spring, and be present at the Christmas banquet. He was a delightful conversationalist. On these occasions, we were always impressed by his learning and his ready wit. In the library, too, we met him in the volumes that he gave to the Villa. It might be a volume of Dante, a book on wildflowers, or a collection of essays. Whatever its subject, it would be annotated along the margin in his quaint, beautiful script with the most apposite remarks. To us, these brief comments of Bishop McGolrick were more illuminating than a whole commentary by another critic.

Happily, the general mourning caused by his death was allayed somewhat when word flashed that a second Bishop of Duluth had been consecrated in the person of Right Reverend John T. McNicholas, OP, then active in Rome as professor at the *Collegio Angelico* [THE DOMINICAN UNIVERSITY IN ROME, ED.] and Assistant to the General of the Dominican Order. Bishop McNicholas arrived in Duluth on November 15, 1918, and was installed on November 17. Although his visits to the College were rarer than those of his predecessor, he manifested his interest in its growth by having letters on Catholic education read on certain Sundays in all the churches of the Diocese and by recommending the education at St. Scholastica. On November 14, 1920, he blessed and baptized our Chapel bell, donated by Mr. and Mrs. Patrick Agnew. On this occasion the beautiful bell stood in the Villa corridor, where the Sisters and students gathered. Mr. and Mrs. Agnew

were sponsors at its baptism, and, when the ceremonies were ended, the Bishop explained all its symbolism and the message the bell should convey to us whenever it was rung. Memorable also were his scholarly addresses at the academic commencements. Hearing them, we rejoiced that Divine Providence had blessed our Diocese and our College, both still in their relative infancy, by giving them another zealous and learned Bishop.

BUILDINGS AND AESTHETIC IMPROVEMENTS
At the beginning of the 1920s several conditions in the school pointed to the need for new buildings. The increase in academic students made more space an obvious necessity. Hence, in 1920 one of the lateral wings of the Villa was enlarged to provide a second story for the garage, a new kitchen, several classrooms, and a chapel with a seating capacity of 260 persons. A current issue of the *Villa Quarterly* describes the chapel as "quiet and prayerful . . . finished in ivory and gray with hand decoration."

The faculty had long been doing excellent work in music and dramatics but had no adequate stage on

Sister Agatha Gruetter and students of the Conservatory of Music

which to practice or present their performances. In the spring of 1921 a gymnasium was built. Its scenic stage, seating equipment, and dressing room made it useful also as an auditorium, a purpose that it served for many years. After its completion two lay teachers were added to the faculty: a competent instructor of physical education [MISS GERALDINE BARRY, ED.] and a distinguished musicologist [MISS CECELIA RAE BERRY, ED.]. The College catalog of 1921 now added a twelve-page supplement entitled *Conservatory of Music*. Its curricula for Pianoforte, Voice, Violin, and Theory foreshadow the high standards that the school has since maintained in all of these departments of music. Also, the *Quarterlies* of 1920 and 1921 contain enthusiastic references to the Chapel and gymnasium, to movies, stage plays, student choir, musicals, etc. Clearly, the value to the school of these new buildings, in the way of convenience and aesthetic pleasure, was very great indeed. As yet, however, they caused no appreciable increase in the enrollment of the College department.

An early music room at Villa Sancta Scholastica

The 1929 graduating class of The College of St. Scholastica

FOUR-YEAR COLLEGE

During the first twelve years of its existence, St. Scholastica was regarded by its students as a junior college. The girls shared almost everything except their class instruction in common with the academics. True, the College students had their own prefect and their own social room, but they walked the same corridors, ate in the same dining halls, followed the same pattern, and were subject to the same direction as the academics. Scholastically they were important. In other respects, their importance was overshadowed by the academics, who were four times their number.

No doubt these conditions were natural and logical while the department remained small. But they made it difficult to "sell" the school to prospective freshmen, who wished to attend a college that was autonomous, not merely an adjunct of an academy. And although the enrolled collegiates loved the Villa, they probably were not immune to like ideas. At all events, in the summer of 1924, when it was announced that henceforth St. Scholastica would be a four-year college with

Students arrive at Villa Sancta Scholastica.

its own dean and a separate section of the building designated for college use only, their enthusiasm spread like a small conflagration. The enrollment of 1924 tripled that of 1923. The reaction of the collegiates to the changes is expressed in a paragraph written by one of them for the "College Chronicle," printed in the autumn number of the *Villa Quarterly* of 1924. It reads:

Everything is wonderful; we are a college in the true sense of the word. We have eighty-six students (the official number is sixty-eight). We are entirely free from the academics. We have our own floor, more than twice as many classrooms and our own private refectory. Our library has been enlarged and, to tip the top, we are a self-governing body. We have formed an Association which is collegiate exclusively. . . . The College Players have begun to practice "Peg O' My Heart" and "Quality Street."

Bishop Welch

An event of signal importance for the Community and its College occurred when the Right Reverend Thomas

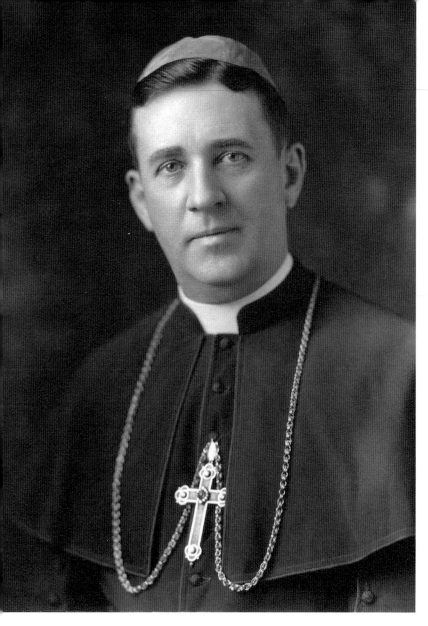

Bishop Thomas Welch, third Bishop of the Diocese of Duluth, (1926 – 1959)

From that time onward, the students were privileged to assist at the Holy Mass, which he celebrated on the formal opening day of the College in October, and to meet him at the formal reception before the Christmas Banquet; and these three occasions—the opening of the College, the formal reception, and Commencement—have been and are, for both faculty and students, the highlights of the school year.

The universal esteem of the student body for Bishop Welch was expressed in a letter recently written by one who attended St. Scholastica from 1927 to 1931. She writes:

> Bishop Welch was very informal. He came quite often to St. Scholastica when I was a student there, sometimes with distinguished visitors, sometimes bringing books, magazines, rare prints, etc. He drove his own car, and we students liked that; it seemed so democratic. He was always friendly and approachable, seeming interested in everybody. How thrilled we students would be when we happened to meet the Bishop on one of these visits, and he would remember our names and ask about our studies, our hometown, or some such. I think his universal kindness helped to perpetuate among the students the atmosphere of friendliness and democracy said to be a special characteristic of our College.

Welch, formerly Chancellor of the Archdiocese of St. Paul and Vicar General under Archbishop Dowling, was appointed by the Holy Father to succeed Bishop McNicholas, who had been named Archbishop of Cincinnati, Ohio. Bishop Welch was installed as Bishop of Duluth on February 4, 1926. He paid his first visit to the College on February 23 and on June 12 presided at our first four-year College graduation, when two young women received the A. B. degree [FRANCES SARAZIN AND

From the first, Bishop Welch was interested in the progress of the school and gave much time and thought to its development. It was under his enlightened guidance that the Sisters, in the fall of 1927, planned and executed the completion of the administration building later known as Tower Hall. He manifested a like interest in all subsequent improvements. His counsel was often sought, and, though it was unobtrusively given, it always proved to be practical and wise.

Tower Hall after the addition of 1927

THE FOUR-YEAR COLLEGE APPROVED BY MINNESOTA

Until 1927 the senior college was only tentatively approved by the University of Minnesota. That year, under date of February 16, a statement was obtained from the University declaring: "Students who take major sequences in departments in which majors are offered will be admitted to the graduate school of the University of Minnesota." A few days later a letter came from the Education Department of the State containing the following assurance: "Such students as have received the bachelor's degree from The College of St. Scholastica and have followed fifteen semester hours of Education with at least thirty hours of Observation and Practice Teaching in high school will receive from the Department of Public Instruction the Minnesota State High School Certificate."

It must not be assumed that these privileges were granted without continuous effort on the part of the Sisters. The first two graduates of St. Scholastica had re-

ceived their teachers' diplomas from a Wisconsin State Normal School before coming to the College, but the graduates of later years were dependent for certification on the Minnesota University and the State Department. Clearly then, the above decisions by the University and the Department of Public Instruction were a *sine qua non* for both the College and its graduates. Like every other advantage, they were obtained by "prayer and work," the Benedictine key to all material and spiritual achievement.

TOWER HALL

Excavation for completing the frontal unit of the administration building began on March 25, 1927. The addition was a five-story structure, 240 feet in length, giving the school a generous measure of sorely needed space. On March 25, 1928, it was finished, and the College students moved proudly into what they considered the "more stately mansions," leaving their vacated quarters to the academics.

A student recreation room in Tower Hall

THE *VILLA QUARTERLY*

From 1911 to 1928 the *Villa Quarterly* was the literary and news organ of the College. During all its life it remained a jewel of consistency in format, size, and organization. Its forty-eight pages began with about twenty pages of serious matter—essays, biography, fiction, interspersed with short poems. Then followed in order two or three pages of editorials on questions of interest to the students, a page or two of criticism on magazines received from other schools, a rather lengthy College chronicle, other current news in six to eight pages, and, at the end, a column labeled "Fact and Fun," "Jokes," or "Humor." The magazine must have functioned to the benefit of many persons, since as many as twenty-five or thirty contributed to some of its issues. In general, the prose articles are commendable, giving evidence on the one hand of careful editing; on the other, of creative work done by the students themselves.

As is usual in amateur publications, most of the "poets" are undeserving of that name, though a few are skillful versifiers. Scattered throughout the humor column are some clever puns, as that of the student who concluded: "All the players in the basketball tournament must be Scots, since the game was so close." Verbal slips are choice pabulum for the jokers: a student in Medieval History tells that "when the Anglo Saxons invaded Britain, they drove the Celts into whales." An instructor in mathematics asks his class to "go through the board before erasing it." The professor of clinical psychology announces that she "had to send to the hospital for a brain because there is none in the College."

IV. Standardization

MEMBERSHIP IN THE NORTH CENTRAL ASSOCIATION

In September 1931 when the enrollment mounted to 104, a new goal appeared above the administrative horizon: other small colleges were members of the North Central Association; why should not St. Scholastica apply for membership? Immediately the suggestion took on substance,

and machinery was set in motion to ready the College for an examination by the Board of Review of the Association. The College song *"Vivat!"* was selected by an all-school contest. New books were purchased in great number, and the library was completely cataloged and standardized in accordance with the system of the Dewey Decimal Classification; new equipment was installed; the faculty was increased. In October the application blanks were requisitioned, and during the months of November and December, the dean and registrar were robbing proverbial beauty sleep to answer questionnaires on the College: its housing facilities, its enrollment, its admission practices, its faculty, its library, and a dozen others. A lengthy questionnaire was answered also for the Academy, which was used as a teacher-training center for the graduates of the College. As the Academy had been accredited by the University of Minnesota since 1912, the Association asked that its report be sent to the University's Educational School, where it would be canvassed by Mr. Boardman and Mr. Shumway and, if recommendable, would be forwarded by them in good time to Mr. Phillips, Chairman of the North Central Association's Commission on Secondary Schools.

VIVAT! VIVAT! ST. SCHOLASTICA

Melody (adapted) by Reynaldo Hahn
Lyrics by Sister Loretta Sheehan

Vivat! Vivat! St. Scholastica.
To thy fame a tribute raise.
Fount of learning, forge of friendship,
Home of happy college days.

Chorus;
Pledge we our faith to alma mater,
Pledge to her our heart and hand.
Where e'er we bide, she'll be our guide.
We will praise her throughout the land,
We will praise her throughout the land.

II
Lakes and hills and spreading campus,
All thy nat'ral charms we love.
And we glory in thy greatness
Bless'd with favors from above.

III
When, in faith and knowledge grounded,
Enter we the world of strife,
May thy counsels, strong and holy,
Aid us in our course through life.

While all this preparatory work was going on, every Sister of the Community, both at home and on the missions, had joined in a campaign of prayer that God would bless the undertaking and make it fruitful for Christian education. On December 13, 1931, all the questionnaires were sent in. The work was finished; prayer would do the rest.

Badminton was a regular part of the Physical Education classes in the early 1930s.

On February 21, 1932, Reverend Alphonse Schwitalla, S. J., Dean of the Graduate School of St. Louis University, was sent by the North Central Association to examine the College. He spent two days on the campus, conferring with the administration and faculty, visiting classes, meeting student groups, and comparing what he found with the

answers in the College questionnaires. Asked before he left if he thought St. Scholastica would get on the North Central, he replied, "Yes, provided the Secondary School Commission acts favorably on your Academy. The teacher-training center must be admitted first."

As the academic questionnaire had been canvassed and reported "Satisfactory!" several weeks before this time, the Sisters were now entirely confident of success. What then was their dismay on learning less than a fortnight before the final meeting that it had not been received by Mr. Phillips. Going to the University, where a search was instituted, they discovered that the precious questionnaire, signed and recommended by the two canvassers and accompanied by a gracious letter from Mr. Shumway, had been stored with other papers in the University's educational files, most likely by an unskilled office hand. Hastily they dispatched it to Mr. Phillips, hoping to still anticipate the Commission's deadline. Ten days later, on March 17, 1932, the dean and the secretary, attending the meeting in Chicago, thrilled at this announcement: "The College of St. Scholastica with her attached high school is admitted to membership in the North Central Association of Colleges and Secondary Schools."

After a second examination made in January 1933 by Dr. E. H. Cameron, Professor of Educational Psychology at Indiana University, the approval was made official. The College became an active member of the North Central Association and was henceforth nationally recognized as a degree-granting institution.

Student nurses board the bus in front of Tower Hall to go to St. Mary's Hospital for their training in the 1930s.

EXAMINERS' REPORTS

The twenty-three pages of typewritten matter contained in the reports of Father Schwitalla and Doctor Cameron touch on many aspects of their visits. The former gives some helpful recommendations toward improvement in "Endowment" and "Class Organization." On the whole, however, the reports are so laudatory that it seems

The cottage in Maryglade was ready for students who needed a place to relax (January 1931).

advisable to refer a possible doubter to the College archives, where they may be examined at first hand.

Father Schwitalla found the buildings "most impressive and dignified, erected with a keen sense of the majestic in architecture and the beautiful in design," the furniture and equipment "in superior taste and the air of refinement and culture noteworthy," the girls "alive and eager in their response" to his address—prepared for every humorous, historical, or political reference . . . the instruction outstanding . . . the faculty "giving evidence of a cosmopolitan spirit and an intense interest in the intellectual" . . . the library of 12,000 volumes "up-to-date."

Dr. Cameron made no recommendations but stated that those made by the previous examiner had been fulfilled. According to his report, "the instruction is almost uniformly excellent. The classrooms and library "give evidence of the studious habits of the girls and the fine moral tone of the institution," . . . "music, art, nursing, and home economics are being maintained at a very high level," and finally, "the grounds and buildings of this institution meet the standards better than any other visited."

Mr. Shumway's letter to the Commission on Secondary Schools, though not detailed in explanation, is no less commendatory. He reports that "the high school has been accredited to the University of Minnesota since 1912," and concludes his letter by stating, "It is my judgment that in equipment, in staff, and in general attitude of student body, it ranks among the best."

ORGANIZATION AND GROWTH

During the years immediately following the admission of the College to the North Central Association, new projects quickened in the academic soil like seedlings under the spring rains. The year 1932 was an *annus mirabilis* in this respect. Practically every month saw new accomplishments in organization. On January 13 the College

Students congregated in the Alpha Chi room on the ground floor of Tower Hall.

newspaper, *Scriptorium*, published its first issue, and the next month a basic course in Western Culture was begun. In March the College formed a chapter of Kappa Gamma Pi, national honor society for Catholic Women's colleges. During the same month, St. Scholastica joined the American and the Minnesota College Associations. In April the faculty introduced the National Comprehensive Examinations for sophomores and organized the regular Thursday Convocations. In May the Athletic Association was inaugurated, and Maryglade Park was developed as a recreational center on the campus. In October the Speech Department formed a chapter of the Alpha Psi Omega, a national society for the encouragement of dramatics, and the College organized the St. Agnes Honor Society and a Student Council. In November the students held their first political rally—Republican vs. Democrat. In December the first Senior Comprehensives were announced.

Although less spectacular in organizations than 1932, the years 1933 to 1935 inclusive were notable in other ways. In 1933 a fire that caused damage to the interior of the student nurses' home at Sacred Heart Institute became the occasion for the remodeling of the building and the construction of an attractive five-story addition fronting toward Third Street. This new wing contained reception rooms, an auditorium, a library,

With the new addition and remodeling,
Sacred Heart Institute was renamed St. Mary's Hall.

private rooms, and an elevator, thus providing a pleasant and convenient home for the 120 student nurses of St. Mary's Hospital and the College. Being now to all appearances a new structure, the "Institute" was given a new name, St. Mary's School of Nursing, or, the shorter name, St. Mary's Hall.

To provide their resident students with opportunities to enjoy occasional outings near Minnesota's lovely waters, the Sisters, in 1934, purchased Shamrock Lodge, a resort at Three Lakes, about thirty miles distant from the College. The Lodge property is well wooded and, therefore, private. It has a Shrine of Our Lady, a boathouse, and a roomy cottage, equipped in every way to accommodate weekend groups of ten or twelve. Its next-door neighbor, the St. Jean Baptiste Parish Club, has a swimming beach that the girls are free to use. Sunday Mass is offered at the "Club" or by arrangement in the cottage or before the shrine. Shamrock Lodge is a popular resort in spring and summer.

Two events that brought rejoicing to every person on the campus occurred the first semester of 1935. On January 11 His Holiness Pope Pius XI named Reverend Patrick Byrnes, the College chaplain, a Domestic Prelate with the title Right Reverend Monsignor. On March 6 the Honorable James Farley, Postmaster General of the United States, authorized The College of St. Scholastica to open its own post office. A Sister who was a lay student at the time remembers the excitement attending both of these events, and of the latter says: "For a week or so the mail was delivered from the bursar's office. On the opening day, I think the entire College went at each delivery to ask for mail. Naturally, many of us were disappointed; but everyone who got a first-day letter was as jubilant as a bibliophile receiving a first issue of a famous book."

MEMBERSHIP IN AMERICAN ASSOCIATION OF COLLEGIATE SCHOOLS OF NURSING

Since the College had been offering a degree course in nursing for several years before 1936, it seemed desirable in that year to obtain membership in a recently formed association for collegiate nurses. Interest in the project was doubtless heightened when the Catholic University of America's nursing unit, of which a Sister-graduate of St. Scholastica was the founder and dean [SISTER OLIVIA GOWAN, ED.], became a charter member of the Association. In January 1936 the College answered the usual questionnaires and sent them to Columbia University, the headquarters of the organization. Shortly afterwards, Miss Isabel M. Stewart, one of the leaders of the movement, paid a brief visit to the College. On June 9, 1936, Miss Elizabeth Burgess came to examine the educational setup in nursing at St. Mary's Hospital and the offerings of the College in science, literature, and the arts. Following her visit, the president of St. Scholastica [MOTHER AGNES SOMERS, ED.] received a letter from the secretary of the organization stating that The College of St. Scholastica was admitted to active membership in the American Association of Collegiate Schools of Nursing.

St. Scholastica was one of the first colleges in the country to achieve this distinction. Since the approval of the Association caused many more prospective nurses to register in the degree sequence at the College, the three-year cadet nursing program was dropped in September 1937, not to be resumed until 1944, when America was suffering from a shortage of trained nurses after World War II.

College of St. Scholastica students could enjoy outings to Shamrock Lodge at Three Lakes.

St. Scholastica students were excited by the opening of a post office on campus, March 1935.

Science was an important part of the curriculum in the 1930s.

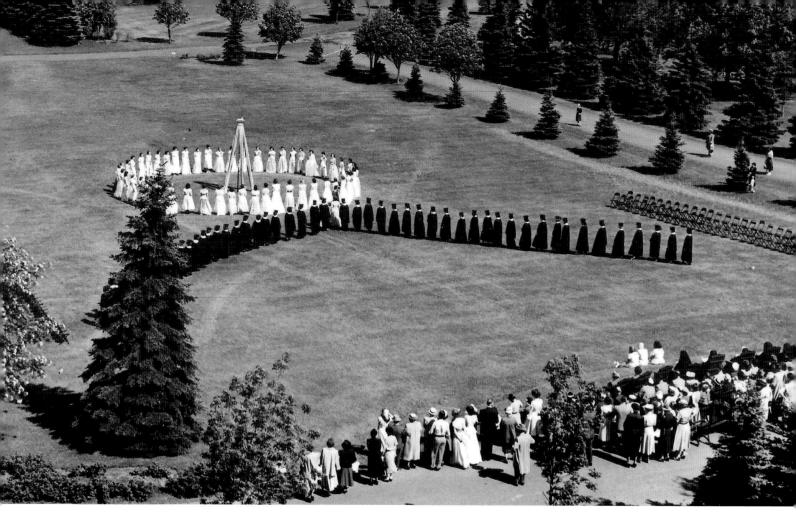

Juniors and Seniors took part in the "Weaving of the Standards" as part of Commencement beginning in 1936.

SYMBOLIC CUSTOMS

On Friday of Commencement Week 1936 the campus below Tower Hall was, for the first time, the scene of a symbolic pageant, which has now become traditional. Its central theme is the "Weaving of the Standards" by the graduates of the current year. When the seniors, arrayed in formals and escorted by the juniors, are assembled around a high pledge-pole erected at the center of the mall, a chosen representative of the Class explains the symbolism of the "weaving," connecting it with some important event in the history of the College, as for instance, "The Coming of Benedictine Nuns to Minnesota, the Opening of the Villa, the Spread of Christian Education in the Diocese of Duluth." Then

follows in rhythmic dance the interlacing of the gold and purple strands around the pledge-pole. At its conclusion, there comes a dramatic silence while the seniors pass the colors to their junior escorts to signify that now they must carry on, keeping high the standards of Alma Mater.

On the first of October of the same year, the entire student body, inspired by a similar enthusiasm for their College, expressed their desire to attain as far as possible the perfect woman envisioned in the "Scholastican Ideal." To achieve this end, they chose by suffrage the following directives, which they designated the "Nine Ideals": Regard for the Spiritual, Sincerity in Word and Act, Love of Scholarship, Loyalty, Courtesy, Initiative,

Friendliness, Appreciativeness, and Poise. Every spring since then, the nine seniors who are thought to best typify these ideals are elected by a secret ballot of faculty and students, and each of the winners is cited for distinction at the Honors Convocation and is given a special page in the yearbook, the *Towers*. It is understood, of course, that the nine electees are not the only beneficiaries of the custom. Everyone who strives for an ideal is a winner. Idealism, like virtue, is to some extent its own reward.

BUILDING EXPANSION

When much greater building space became imperative in 1936, the Sisters engaged a company of architects [O'MEARA, HILLS, AND QUICK, ED.] from St. Louis to draw plans and specifications for a residence hall, an auditorium, a chapel/library, and two connecting cloister walks. At the same time, the grounds around the buildings were blueprinted, and plans were drawn for the gate entrance from Kenwood Avenue to the campus. Contracts were let on July 1, 1936, and, as the entire construction was scheduled for completion in exactly two years, the work began at once.

The Michigan Club in 1937-1938

Skating was always a popular pastime at the College.

In the spring of 1937 significant names were chosen for these buildings. The war provoked by Hitler was raging in Europe, and the Holy Father was making constant pleas for peace. So the Sisters decided to place their Chapel under the patronage of the Blessed Mother and to give it the title "Our Lady Queen of Peace." Near the emplacement of the auditorium is a granite cliff whose sides and summit are encircled by a grove or hurst of trees. This picturesque feature inspired the name "Rockhurst" for the auditorium; and the new residence hall and training center of the College was called "Stanbrook" after a celebrated English abbey of Benedictine nuns. The background history of this little group of Sisters is always interesting to new students as well as to the many friends and sightseers who yearly come to visit St. Scholastica. In brief outline, the story is as follows: The nuns were organized as a religious community in 1629 and made their first foundation at Cambrai in Spanish Flanders. Among the members were Dame Gertrude More and her two cousins, all descendants of St. Thomas More. At Cambrai they were

Stanbrook Hall when new in 1938

directed by Benedictine monks coming from England. Here Dame Gertrude marked the path of the true contemplative in her book, *Confessiones Amantis*; here, for more than a century and a half, the community continued its peaceful life, devoting itself to the liturgy and to publications. In 1793 the French Revolutionists seized their house and property and carried them to a revolutionary prison at Compiegne to await execution by the guillotine. Saved two years later by the timely downfall of Robespierre, they escaped as refugees to England, where they were received by English Benedictine monks and helped by secular friends. In 1838 the little community purchased a small English manor called Stanbrook Hall and gradually built around it the now famous Stanbrook Abbey. Though still dedicated to the contemplative life, the nuns receive for education within the cloister a number of young women. Stan-

brook Abbey has gained a reputation for excellence in art [AND LITERATURE, ED.].

In September of 1937 the College registered 358 students, and enthusiasm ran high. But the residence halls were so congested that the community had to rent a large dwelling on Skyline Boulevard where a number of Sisters could be housed at night, commuting back and forth by bus. A student at the time, recalling the crowded condition that prevailed, says: "That fall the place was so jammed with college and high school girls that we almost pushed out the windows. But we didn't mind the crowding; new ideas were constantly taking form, new buildings were going up, and the thrill of the unexpected colored everything."

Undoubtedly, the Sisters felt otherwise. We can imagine how welcome were the changes when Rockhurst Auditorium was sufficiently completed by the middle of

December 1937 to function as a banquet hall and program center for the twentieth annual Christmas celebration in honor of the Bishop, and when the high school students were permitted to move to Stanbrook Hall in January 1938.

As in the building of Tower Hall, construction on the grounds kept pace with construction on the masonry. Hence, on July 20, 1938, when the Chapel/library and cloister walks were turned over to the owners, paved walks, green terraces, and brilliant flower borders around the new buildings were in order, and the fine gate development with stone posts, central mall plantings, and double driveway was finished. The extensive building program was complete.

CONTRIBUTION OF THE COLLEGE TO THE PAROCHIAL SCHOOLS

Besides preparing its graduates for teaching and other professional jobs, the College has done much to prepare teachers for the many parish schools staffed by the Community. In 1920 and 1921 young Sisters in considerable numbers began to register at Duluth State Teachers' College, where they were given a year of advanced standing for work done in the College, the credits of the second year to be earned in normal school courses. At the time, there existed—as there still exists—in the Constitutional Provisions of the Public School System of Minnesota, an opinion delivered by the Attorney General of the State on May 23, 1904, that "the wearing of the garb of a religious body by teachers while teaching in the public schools is prohibited" (and that) "the prohibition applies to practice teachers in teachers' colleges" (*Laws of Minnesota* Ch.1, Sec. 4, 4).

Because most of the Sisters were superior students in their classes, but mainly, no doubt, because many of them had already taught a year

As the College grew, the old library in Tower Hall became inadequate for students' needs.

A single dorm room in Tower Hall

Students used the library in Tower Hall for research and studying.

Many special college ceremonies took place in the new Chapel of Our Lady Queen of Peace.

The College of St. Scholastica education majors did their student teaching in area schools. This woman taught at Sacred Heart School.

or more, the authorities of Teachers' College arranged that the eight credits in cadet teaching, which were an essential part of the second year's program, might be done in the parochial schools under the supervision of the head of the Education Department at Duluth Teachers' College. This plan had been followed for a year when the supervisor in charge of the classes announced regretfully that he was not allowed to present the eight credits earned by the Sisters as Practice Teaching but would present them as Theory of Education.

Since the Sisters wanted certification and not necessarily educational theory, they transferred to the Teachers' College in Superior, Wisconsin, where no anti-garb law prevailed. There, as in Duluth, the teaching was excellent; the teachers, appreciative. The Sisters received one or two years' credit for work completed in the College,

according as they registered for the two- or the three-year program. Most of them attended only during summer sessions, commuting by streetcar from one of their mission houses in Duluth. The long trip to Superior was inconvenient. So when, in 1934, it was discovered that the statute books of Minnesota contained other opinions of the Attorney General that seemed to circumvent the anti-garb law, the Supervisor of the parish school teachers once more applied to the Teachers' College in Duluth for the certification of her teachers. In response, the Duluth Teachers' College, reversing its former policy, not only gave credit for the cadet teaching, but allowed it to be done in the parochial schools under the supervision of the Education Department of the College.

Up to the year 1950, when St. Scholastica introduced the degree program in Elementary Education, 118 Sisters were certified by the Teachers' Colleges of Duluth and Superior. After graduating from these institutions, those who had not already completed their liberal arts courses again took work at St. Scholastica in order to obtain the Bachelor of Science or Bachelor of Arts degree.

V. To Wider Fields

OPENING OF THE CHAPEL AND LIBRARY

The *Duluth Catholic Register* in its issue of August 21, 1938, contains a news item on the consecration of the main altar of the Chapel of Our Lady Queen of Peace by His Excellency, the Most Reverend Thomas A. Welch, on August 1, 1938. The same item gives the following details of the Solemn Pontifical High Mass celebrated on the newly consecrated altar on August 15:

Preceding the Mass, His Excellency blessed the Chapel. The procession of the Most Reverend Bishop, the Right Reverend Monsignor, and the Reverend Clergy, led by the crossbearer, acolytes, and assistants, passed from the sacristy through the nave of the Chapel to the main entrance under the Great East window. Here, facing toward the Chapel, the impressive rite began with the singing of the "Miserere." His Excellency, accompanied by the crossbearer and acolytes, then passed through the north cloister walk into the Angelus Garden, around the north and south transepts, and through the south court and blessed with appropriate liturgical ceremony the walls of the church.

At the Pontifical Mass, the Rt. Rev. Patrick Byrnes acted as assistant priest; the Rev. Patrick Joseph Truman, OSB, and the Rev. William E. Guilfoyle, as deacons; the Rev.

Stanbrook Hall and the Chapel of Our Lady Queen of Peace were well landscaped by the early 1940s.

A "book brigade" moved books from the old library in Tower Hall to the new library before the start of school in 1938.

Lawrence Glenn as subdeacon; the Rev. Myron Currie and the Rev. David Gleason, as masters of ceremonies. The sermon was preached by the Rev. Joseph Cashen.

Before the opening of the College in September, the 18,000 volumes that then constituted the book collection had been shelved in the present library. The released space in Tower Hall and the more expansive quarters in the new buildings led to an increase in the enrollment, and this in turn occasioned further change in the curriculum. The word "further" is used advisedly. All through the period 1925-1950, curricular expansion was a marked characteristic of liberal arts colleges throughout the Midwest. The following chronology of the academic development at St. Scholastica during the

quarter century is evidence that it was in harmony with the general trend.

EXPANSION OF THE COLLEGE CURRICULUM, 1925-1950

Up to the year 1926, the faculty prepared their graduates for secondary school teaching of a general character. When the urge for specialized teaching came in, they began to supplement their earlier offerings by sequences in special teaching subjects. Thus, in 1926 they introduced a sequence in Home Economics; in 1928 they offered for the first time a degree course in Nursing Education designed for teachers in hospital training schools. Between 1928 and 1936 they introduced six new sequences: Sociology in 1929, Business Education in 1934, Public School Music in 1935. Also in 1935, in order to raise the status of their hospital technicians, they introduced three sequences leading to the Bachelor of Science degree. These were Dietetics, Medical Technology, and Medical Record Librarian. The latter sequence, which was first developed and raised to the degree level at St. Scholastica [BY SISTER

The Home Management House, built in 1939, served Home Economics students until 1991.

PATRICIA THIBADEAU, ED.], was approved in 1935. It has since been adopted by other colleges and universities throughout the country. Graduates of this sequence at St. Scholastica must complete a major in the social sciences as well as a minor in English, library science, or business.

In 1939 the Sisters built a demonstration house for child training, and the following year federal and state agencies approved the College for training of home economics teachers under the Smith-Hughes Act. Graduates of this sequence, upon recommendation of the College, were eligible to receive the High School Standard Special Certificate, which assures better placement opportunities as well as better training for homemakers. In 1940 a substantial frame building was moved to the northeast corner of the athletic field to house three standard bowling alleys, and the catalog announced a minor sequence in physical education. In 1942 the twelve credits in library science formerly required for English teachers in the secondary schools were raised to sixteen, making a minor sequence in library science. Finally, in 1950 the College, following

*Home Economics students
practiced clothing construction in their classes.*

*St. Scholastica students learned etiquette
at banquets such as this Christmas celebration.*

a recommendation of the Minnesota State Department of Education, adopted the degree program in elementary teaching. Within a few years, practically all the other colleges in Minnesota had followed suit.

While most of these sequences are more vocational than the generalized teaching of an earlier date, no extreme departures were made from the liberal arts. Even in nursing, home economics, dietetics, and physical education, the ratio of liberal arts classes to vocational is two to one. It is noteworthy that in the Graduate Record and Honors Examinations, both of which connote a rather high level of cultural competence, students of all the above sequences may, and often do, achieve distinction—a proof that liberal education at St. Scholastica is not neglected.

SECOND WORLD WAR

In September 1941, 457 students registered in the College. Of these, 137 were freshmen (Files of the Registrar). School was moving prosperously, and the Community was planning new development when the tragic news of Pearl Harbor shattered expectations and aroused both

Students found some time to relax in the recreation rooms in Tower Hall.

faculty and students to the urgency of national defense. To the administration's plea for prayer and sacrifice, the students gave magnificent response. Between classes they hurried to the Chapel and raised their voices in petition to the King and Queen of Peace. At recreation periods they set up booths along the corridors to collect for the purchase of war stamps, war bonds, a military jeep. Teachers organized evening courses in first aid and in home nursing. Alumnae "signed up" as Red Cross nurses, nursing aides, WACS, or WAVES; and during the war years at least two alumnae were cited for Distinguished Service. Practically every Sister, lay teacher, and student had a brother, a nephew, or other close relative in the conflict. When word came of a dear one killed or missing, there was universal mourning, yet there was no defeatism. The girls seemed to realize more fully their responsibility as Americans; the administration and faculty realized more fully their duty to give their students the full development of body, mind, and spirit befitting worthy citizens of a great commonwealth.

Most assuredly the saying, "in wartime the intellec-

tual is neglected," was not true at St. Scholastica. In 1941 the Lumen Club purchased four hundred of the best recent works in Catholic studies; the Alumnae, now numbering 2000, began the publication of *The Chattersheet*; the nursing department formed a chapter of Alpha Tau Delta, the official honor society for graduates in the degree course. Also in 1941 the College was given a unique opportunity for further service and development when it was selected by the North Central Association to be one of the twenty-eight colleges working on a cooperative study the Association had organized to test the efficiency of the small colleges of liberal arts. In these studies, each institution was to choose its own area of investigation and to share its findings with the other colleges. The faculty of St. Scholastica chose to work in the area of evaluation. They began by polling their alumnae, from the earliest class in 1926 through the class of 1941, on the values of the courses they had taken at the College and on the effectiveness of their total college education in preparing them to meet the religious, cultural, home, and civic situations they had experienced since graduation. In 1942, on the basis of the answers to the questionnaire, the faculty made changes in their curricular and extracurricular offerings. Certain courses and activities were dropped, others modified or strengthened. There was a tendency to greater stress on general education. In 1943 the annual Faculty Institute was established "to sensitize the administrative and instructional staffs to current trends in higher education." In 1944 the Graduate Record Examination was introduced to determine the strengths and weaknesses of educational performance at St. Scholastica in comparison with the national norms.

Many St. Scholastica graduates began a devotion to the Blessed Mother through participation in the Sodality.

MATERIAL DEVELOPMENTS

Material improvements on the main campus, interrupted at the onset of the war, began again in 1947. In the spring a new Otis elevator filled the empty shaft in Stanbrook Hall, and the flower conservatory was rebuilt. Also a row of electric luminaries was placed along the entrance drive. In the autumn a neat brick cottage arose beside the skating rink. It was built in two sections: the main one, to be a warming place for the skaters; the other, a rendezvous for lovers of the "weed" (cigarettes). On June 15, 1949, a beautiful Cassavant pipe organ was installed in the Chapel of Our Lady Queen of Peace [IT WAS REPLACED WHEN THE CHAPEL WAS RELOCATED IN 1986. ED.].

An organization that will undoubtedly enlarge the material and social opportunities of the College and its students was formed in 1948 when the administration chose its first Advisory Board. This body of a dozen members consists of professional and business men and women and alumnae of the College. For convenience all are residents of Duluth and nearby cities of Minnesota and Wisconsin. The Advisory Board meets once or twice a year to discuss certain matters pertaining to the welfare of the College and its student body.

With the resumption of the cadet nursing program at the hospital in 1944, St. Mary's Hall was found to be inadequate as a residence for the two groups of nurses; in 1945 the first unit of Victory Hall arose at the corner of Fourth Avenue East and Fourth Street in close proximity to the hospital. When it was enlarged in 1950, both groups of nursing students occupied it, and St. Mary's Hall was remodeled to be a convent for the Sisters at the hospital.

A substantial skating house was built in 1947.

Students enjoy a concert in Tower Hall.

Radio Production was added to the Speech Department offerings in the 1940s.

Organizations often held formal teas such as this Initiation Tea in 1945.

In remodeling, the auditorium became an ideal chapel, and the ancient community room and dining room, redolent with memories of the past, reverted to their early uses.

An Unusual Visitor

The completion of Victory Hall and the remodeling of St. Mary's Convent in 1950 have been recorded. Another event of 1950, though it may seem trivial, is so well remembered that it has become historical: on September 13 an unusual visitor came to Maryglade. It was Registration Day. Word of his presence soon flashed among the students. Upperclassmen were elated; freshmen were horrified. Exclaimed the latter: "I think that's terrible! Why do they allow it?" . . . "Terrible?" said the seniors. "Why it's won-der-ful. Think of the distinction it will give us! We're the first college in America to register a bear!"

Research Projects

An opportunity was given St. Scholastica to extend its usefulness when the Most Reverend John T. McNicholas, Archbishop of Cincinnati, Ohio, in 1942 invited the president [Mother Agnes Somers, Ed.] to send two Sisters to the *Institutum Divi Thomae*, a scientific center that he had organized for graduate students preparing to do specialized research. The College accepted this gracious invitation and sent two of its Sister graduates in science [Sister Petra Lenta and Sister Agatha Riehl, Ed.] for three years of study at the *Institutum*. After their return home in 1945 the College equipped a special laboratory for their use. In reporting on their findings during the next seven years, the Sisters state:

> The work we have done is of the nature of basic cancer research. We investigated both normal and abnormal growth, since it is felt that an abnormal growth like that of cancer will be understood only in the light of a more complete knowledge of the myriad delicate reactions which constitute normal growth. Therefore, research tests were made on hundreds of experi-

mental animals, including studies on six different types of cancer, and the analysis of many normal tissues. The studies were chiefly in metabolism, the emphasis being placed on the vital intra-cellular enzymatic reactions. The results of our work were recorded in the several papers published by *Cancer Research*, the official organ of the American Association for Cancer Research. Our experiments were greatly aided by money donations amounting to $10,000 from the Minnesota Cancer Society, the Damon Runyan Foundation, and private benefactors.

During the years 1946 and 1947 two works of value to the school world were produced by members of the College faculty. In 1946 *The History of Legislation Affecting Private Elementary and Secondary Schools* was written by a Sister doing research at Catholic University [Sister Raymond McLaughlin, Ed.]. This work, the first comprehensive study to trace the development of the relationships between the state and private schools, has proved valuable not only to Catholic school administrators but also to several members of the law. A second printing was asked for recently, and, when it appears shortly, the history will be traced to date.

Outdoor exercise such as snowshoeing was important to St. Scholastica students in the 1940s.

August 2nd of the following year saw the publication of the *First Fifteen Years* [by Sister Digna Birmingham, Ed.], an interpretative report of the answers to the questionnaire sent by the College faculty to its alumnae in 1942. The book received acclaim from educators the country over. It was hailed as an initial work on the effectiveness of higher education in Catholic colleges for women. Dean Peik of the College of Education at the University of Minnesota called it "a pilot study" and hoped that many other institutions might be stimulated to promote studies of a similar kind.

In 1951 a second questionnaire was issued to the 890 students who had graduated between 1941 and 1951 in order to determine the effectiveness of the modified program under which they had received their college education. The outcomes of this questionnaire will be published in a forthcoming book being written by the director of the "Studies," [Sister Digna Birmingham, Ed.] and financed by an allotment of $6,500 from the Louis W. and Maud Hill Family Foundation [This report is *A Second Look*, published in 1955. Ed.].

It may be of interest to the reader to learn the nature and purpose of some of the other studies undertaken in the area of evaluation:

Students who lived on campus found opportunities for recreation during the 1940s and 1950s.

Students who lived at home and commuted to school had lunch and conversation in the Day Students' Cafeteria in the 1940s and 1950s.

1. The objectives of the College were subjected to a careful analysis and were restated, in the belief that objectives, clearly understood, serve as a frame of reference in appraising the total program of activities of an institution.

2. A formal system of counseling and a manual of the same were set up to replace the more informal personnel methods of the previous years.

3. A study was made of the various types of examinations in use at the College, and a more uniform system of testing was presented in a brochure on the subject of college examinations.

4. Instructors made complete syllabi of their courses in order to obviate overlapping of subject matter in the classes.

5. An attempt was made to appraise classroom procedures by means of student reaction questionnaires.

6. A large number of the instructors attended summer workshops sponsored by the North Central Association in order to make contact with the representatives from the other co-operating colleges and to gain insight and inspiration from the addresses of outstanding educators.

MEMBERSHIP IN THE AMERICAN ASSOCIATION OF UNIVERSITY WOMEN

An honor of significance came to us in 1951: the College was named a member of the American Association of University Women. While membership in this organization is a mark of intellectual leadership rather than professional efficiency, it places St. Scholastica among the highest-ranking educational institutions for women in the nation. Simultaneously, it gives her graduates an official status as cultural leaders in their environment and in larger fields of intellectual effort.

In announcing the honor to the president [Sister Athanasius Braegelman, Ed.] and dean [Sister Rose O'Donnell, Ed.] of the College, the president of the local chapter said: "The Association of American University

Students in Sister Mary Scholastica Bush's Freshman Rhetoric class in January 1947 learned to do research and prepare note cards.

Women congratulates The College of St. Scholastica on achieving the high standards necessary to membership in the AAUW. We have long realized your high standards, through the capacity for leadership manifested by your alumnae."

LIBRARY SERVICE

No longer are college libraries just attractive storage places for books to be distributed on request. Within the past two decades they have become instructional centers, second only to the classroom. Today teachers and librarians cooperate to promote scholarship by interesting the students in reading matter that formerly did not attract them. In the library service at St. Scholastica this objective, pursued progressively since 1938, now manifests itself in a greatly increased circulation of the deeper types of reading and in the marked growth of the collection.

From the start, the College maintained a rather liberal policy in admitting students to its shelves. The popular fiction and periodical rooms, as well as the general reference room, were accessible to every reader; but for many years the stacks, where the more erudite books are stored, remained closed. Finally, in 1949 the librarians and faculty, convinced that informal browsing among many books is one of the best challenges to culture, voted for an open stack room. Gradually, too, other methods were devised to bring the student and the book together. Among these methods, shelf displays, informal talks on books, bulletin boards, book fairs, and reviews in campus publications were perhaps the most effective. The result? Circulation increased perceptibly from year to year. According to the record cards of 1952,

Students enjoyed using the new library when it opened in 1938.

Sister Katharine McCarthy led St. Scholastica students on a visit to the statue of St. Scholastica behind the College some time in 1943.

sidering many of the faculty department heads are advocates of textbooks, and all the students are expected to consult general and specialized reference material at the school.

In the past twenty years the growth of book resources in college libraries has been phenomenal. St. Scholastica has endeavored to keep pace with the service in this respect too. In 1932, when it was standardized, the library catalog contained 12,000 titles; in 1952 it had 34,500 titles—an average increase of 1,100 books and magazines a year. As in all libraries, the growth has come by budget purchase, by gift, and by bequest. About ninety-five percent of the College collection must be credited to the first method, all

withdrawals from the library for recreational and cultural reading now average 7.05 books per student every month. While this is not the ideal of eight withdrawals a month for small colleges of liberal arts, it is high, con-

purchases being made by the head librarian in consultation with faculty members or committees. Money is often given for new publications by friends or alumnae of the College. For example, in 1942 the

Alumnae Association gave $1,000 for the library; from 1943 to 1953, Miss Alice Lamb, an alumna of Stanbrook Hall, ordered from the book companies all the best current publications in the fields of philosophy and religion. To keep the shelves free for new material, the books with outdated copyrights were discarded when revised printings were acquired. Naturally, this practice does not apply to classic literature—reading matter that has nourished and still nourishes the world's noblest thought. Old favorites retain an honored place among the younger volumes, but mere "learned lumber" is regularly cleared away. As a consequence, St. Scholastica has a fairly good library of well-selected books.

Although most of its collection is due to budgeting, the library has received some very valuable gifts and also some bequests. Instances of the former between 1941 and

Art students in a spacious studio on the top floor of Tower Hall in the 1940s

Games provided recreation for St. Scholastica students, such as these two students pictured in the fall of 1952.

1949 are: a complete edition of The *Oxford English Dictionary*, a Dante set, and a goodly number of rare books and first issues, among them the earliest edition of Samuel Johnson's *English Dictionary*, donated by His Excellency, the Most Reverend Thomas A. Welch; a rare edition of *The Jesuit Relations* in seventy-three volumes donated by Mrs. Wm. Crago; numerous autographed books and sets with special hand tooling and binding, donated by Mrs. Afton Hilton; three hundred volumes of great current value in the study of literature donated by the Right Reverend Monsignor Byrnes; substantial gifts of books donated by Judge Martin Hughes and Dr. E. L. Touhy. A significant bequest received in 1944 was that of the late Reverend John Sholar, who bequeathed his library of 1,200 titles on education and philosophy to the College.

The grounds of the campus of The College of St. Scholastica as it looked when Sister Agnes Somers wrote her account of the history of the College

END OF HISTORY

September 1952 marks the fortieth year of effort by The College of St. Scholastica to educate students in the science and the art of higher education. It marks also the hundredth anniversary of the coming of Benedictine Sisters to America. The date seems a fitting closure to this historical sketch.

SOURCES OF THIS HISTORY FROM 1932 TO 1952

It will be evident to the reader that many sources were drawn upon for the statements and figures cited in the second division of this history. But, memories apart,

Scriptorium and the *Towers* formed the main [sources] of information. Undoubtedly, these two publications gave greater unity and vitality to the College and enlarged the dimensions of its students. For these reasons, they merit commendation.

THE *SCRIPTORIUM*

The *Scriptorium* is a seven-column biweekly newspaper of four pages whose avowed purpose, as expressed in its first issue of January 13, 1932, is: "to work toward the informal dignity of modern journalism, to cooperate with the administration, and to respect the traditions of the College." A casual examination of all issues from 1932 to 1952 tends to show that the paper has kept quite consistently to these aims. No doubt, that is one reason why the *Scriptorium* has rated All-College Honors [Associated Press Collegiate Honors, Ed.] year after year during the twenty years of its existence.

A sampling of the editorials seems to indicate that the student staff has been alert to the international as well as the national problems of the passing years. Subjects like "Live the Mass," "Thanksgiving Food for Thought," "Facism vs. Communism," "Human Lives or Black Market," "Democracy Means What?", "Interracial Justice," "Know the Why of Things," "Rome or Moscow," picked at random, are treated with understanding and conviction.

The news section is alive with names, dates, and color. It deals with occurrences on the local scene, which is entirely as it should be, since such events have an acute personal interest for the students and their families. The coverage is comprehensive. There are items on college expansion, the Blessed Virgin Sodality, examinations and honors, attendance at national and regional meetings, books and published articles of the faculty and students, alumnae news, convocations, club activities, book reviews, music, drama, radio and TV programs produced by the College, fashions, and sports.

Among other elements in the newspaper are verse, feature stories, and jokes. Ten or twelve of the poems in the *Scriptorium* were printed in *Spirit* or *American Anthology of Verse*. Most of them are mere end-rhyming. (Emphatically, poets are not made!) The special features consist of "pithy portraits" of certain students and stories of unusual human interest to the College population. Among the best feature stories are "Jimmy Goes for a Ride with Mary Lu," "Baby Rules the Demonstration House," "Lucky," "The Sophs' Shooting Star," "Jones Discusses Granite and the Weather," "Cr-o-a-k." They are cleverly conceived and humorously written.

Scriptorium staffs such as this one from the 1940s won Sister Agnes Somers' admiration for their excellent writing and professional publications.

Scriptorium *(below)*
and The Towers *(right), the*
two main sources relied upon by
Sister Agnes Somers as she compiled
the original manuscript for
this book in the 1950s

Jokes, though not plentiful, are refreshing. For example, a Duluth printer announces that "Jan Chiapusso, internally known pianist, will appear at The College of St. Scholastica Oct. 26, 1932." An examinee in English Survey writes: "Robert Louis Stevenson married in July, 1881, and on his wedding tour wrote *Travels with a Donkey.*" A columnist wittily remarks: "To wear a college cap successfully, one needs a level head."

The Towers

Next to the *Scriptorium*, the most informative source was the yearbook, the *Towers*. It is a luxurious volume, bound in leather, and filled with artistic photography showing religious leaders; individual pictures of the graduates; winners of the Nine Ideals; club activities; proms and parties; complete junior, sophomore, and freshman groups; formal teas and banquets; buildings; outdoor shrines; garden nooks; athletic scenes, etc. To the writer, *Towers* was indicative and informing; to the alumnae, it will likely be in the future years a fairyland of memories where they will sometimes wander, reviving their days and deeds in college. Like the *Scriptorium*, the *Towers* has captured All-American Honors almost every year since its first issue in 1937.

Part Two:
Artistic

Villa Sancta Scholastica as it looked from 1921 – 1927

Previous page: The statue of St. Scholastica that stood by the entrance of Villa Sancta Scholastica in 1911 now has a home near the road to the Monastery cemetery.

VI. The College Buildings and their Architecture

In September 1909 Villa Scholastica, the initial wing of the College, was erected. Successive additions to this first building were made in 1914, 1919, 1921, and 1928 as the school grew in numbers and completed its transition to a college [SEE APPENDIX D, ED.]. In 1937 and 1938 came a

more extensive expansion, and in 1950 a nurses' residence was built near St. Mary's Hospital. At present, the major buildings comprise Tower Hall, the gymnasium, Stanbrook Hall, Rockhurst Auditorium,

Chapel/library, and Victory Hall. The purpose of the present chapter is to give the relative emplacement of these buildings and tell something of their architecture.

The gymnasium, which resembles an English chapel, has graced the grounds since 1921.

Tower Hall (after the 1927 addition) and the bus that took nursing students to St. Mary's Hospital

SCHOLASTIC AND RESIDENCE HALLS

THE VILLA

The earliest of these structures, later a part of Tower Hall, was built in late English Tudor style, its large size and massive walls of blue trap granite giving it a kinship with its environment. The name *Villa* soon became familiar to Duluthians, and, although both buildings and surroundings have long since outgrown their rural character, it is still often used to designate the College. [PHOTO ON PAGE 56, ED.]

THE GYMNASIUM

The gymnasium, erected at the west of the Villa in 1921, proclaims its affinity with the earlier building by its blue-trap walls, its horizontal lines, and its arched windows. Other features—stone belfry, stepped gable and ivied walls—suggest an English Derivative style such as may be seen in pictures of Early American churches. Indeed, many persons, viewing it only from the outside, will immediately exclaim: "What a charming English chapel!"

Interiorly it has all the marks of a gymnasium and is completely equipped to function as such. Its whole space is clear of obstruction except for the stage at its south end. Until 1938 the building served for both auditorium and gymnasium. When it was used as an auditorium, the high stage provided a demonstration floor; when used as gymnasium, it provided space underneath for the storage of seats. [PHOTO ON PAGE 57, ED.]

TOWER HALL

In 1928 the Villa was completed by the addition of a central facade and a wing duplicating the first building. The result was a structure with a north to south axis of 375 feet, its great length relieved by turrets at either end, recessed fenestration, and the Tudor towers flanking the facade. Viewed from the front, Tower Hall is most imposing. Yet its front aspect is no criterion of its size, for lateral wings, built in 1914, 1919, and 1921, almost double its extent. The building stands high on a slope facing east. It is approached by three flights of stone steps: the first two ascending from the campus to a terrace of granite construction, crossing before the entrance and the towers, and the third flight arising from the terrace to the threshold.

Throughout the building a white limestone of fine but strong texture is used in contrast to the somber blue trap. It composes the Tudor balustrade around the terrace, the gable cross, the stately portico, and the wealth of carved symbolism on the main facade. Still further contrast is achieved by means of metalwork and color. Ornamental iron lanterns placed on standards rise above the evergreen plantings on the terrace, while bronze over-doors and grilles, set with large bronze medals of St. Benedict, impart a note of brilliance to the portal.

Inside the double door, a small vestibule in Kesota [WINONA, ED.] marble admits to a spacious foyer. This foyer, with its vestibule and a reception room at either side, occupies the fifty feet between the Tudor towers

and is twenty feet wide. The reception rooms at right and left extend inward along the side walls, thus cutting the central section into a tau cross. The arms of the cross become hallways leading to the tower parlors. Three other features of the lobby—tiled floors, paneled walls, and parget ceiling—show a variety of imaginative treatment. Colorful Nemadji tile, produced in Minnesota, gives a local character to the floors; paneling in wormy chestnut, fumed to antique brown, gives serenity to the walls; ceilings, molded into patterns of the Tudor rose and patriarchal cross in gold, red, and royal blue, are reminiscent of the High Middle Ages. Other decorative elements increasing the originality of the lobby are the six doors of Florentine glass, the lead

The foyer of Tower Hall

*Students used the sun porches in Tower Hall
for recreation and studying.*

*A cloister walk connects Tower Hall to the Chapel
and library and to Stanbrook Hall.*

lines of which are wrought into symbols of the Blessed Trinity, the Alpha and Omega, the Circle of Eternity, the Star of Israel, the Tree of Life, and the Ladder of Jacob.

Two features that give the Tudor character to the main corridor are its great length and its wide stairway. The corridor extends through the axis of the building, thus affording abundant wall space for a continuous scheme of decorative treatment. Directly across from the lobby is a Tudor stairway to which has been added these contemporary features: midway between each two levels of the building, the landing of the double staircase projects outward to include a pleasant sunporch; and on the highest landing the two flights unite inward to form a gallery looking out upon a triple-windowed bay.

CLOISTER WALKS

Everyone will agree that cloister walks add beauty to a group of buildings, but beauty alone would not justify their presence in a building plan. "Handsome is as handsome does"; hence, they always serve both practical and aesthetic purposes. The College has a west and an east cloister walk, called so because of their positions at the east and west sides of the cloister garden. Both walks are completely walled in, heated by direct radiation, and built with large arched windows, thus giving a maximum of sunlight or at least of comfort to those who pass between the buildings in cold or rainy weather.

The west walk connects the faculty wing and the Chapel; the east walk, connecting Tower Hall, the Chapel, and Stanbrook Hall is two hundred-eighty feet in length and is furnished with benches, fern boxes, and radiator covers, all artistically made of white oak, polychromed to match the woodwork of the Chapel. Externally also this cloister walk is functional and beautiful. At the point where it connects with Tower Hall, St. Cloud granite in gray, rose, and buff supplants the blue trap. At the same point, the style of architecture changes to Romanesque. However, both changes have been treated so effectively that the result is natural and pleasing. Below the cloister walk, a paved esplanade, beginning at Tower Hall, passes before the Chapel and extends to Stanbrook Hall. This long terrace is held by a retaining wall of St. Cloud granite with a balustrade of Indiana limestone.

Graduating students process along the esplanade from Tower Hall, passing before the Chapel, on their way to the graduation ceremony in Rockhurst Auditorium.

Stanbrook Hall, built in 1938, was a girls' high school and is now St. Scholastica Monastery.

STANBROOK HALL

This building runs north and south in direct line with Tower Hall. Built of St. Cloud granite with white limestone trim, its two hundred thirty feet of length and its fine approach create a balance for the building at the north end of the quadrangle. It is a five-story building, strong in mass, yet exhibiting in its general appearance that sense of verticality said to be a characteristic of our national style. But while it is American and modern, it displays the influences of the past in the symbolism on its facade.

The decorative scheme of this facade might very well convey the purpose of Stanbrook Hall: that of educating young women in the Christian way of life. The upper part of the facade is adorned with a gable cross and the Early Christian symbols of Faith, Hope, Charity, Mortification, and Purity of Heart carved in deep relief. No less significant are six symbols on the frieze above the entrance doors: the sunflower, the butterfly, the wild rose, the daisy, the scales, and the palm branch, signifying in their respective order Obedience, Progress in Goodness, Love of Neighbor, Sincerity, Justice, and Fortitude.

In harmony with the other buildings, Stanbrook Hall has a terrace of like construction, with three flights of granite steps, a stone balustrade, and ornamental iron lanterns. The entrance doors, recessed about six feet within a stone framework, are made from golden oak; their lower parts designed in concentric oak panels; their upper parts, in eggshell glass of white, green, and gold.

THE AUDITORIUM

Rockhurst Auditorium runs due west from Stanbrook Hall; the building is four stories high and one hundred thirty feet long. Frankly American and modern, it expresses its use externally by an enclosed circular staircase with a domed roof. Within, it is spacious, having an easy seating capacity of nine hundred persons. The stage, which is suitable for large casts and choruses, is furnished with complete equipment for colored lights and moving picture presentation. There is provision also for the installation of a pipe organ.

Like other buildings, the auditorium makes use of symbolic motifs. Some of these are tacit and modern, others hallowed by time. Symbols used to designate the abundant gifts of nature to Minnesota are trout to represent her lakes, great and small; moccasin flowers and pine cones to signify the wealth of her woods; and snowflakes to indicate her hardy northern climate. But since an auditorium has mainly an aesthetic purpose, masks, buskins, and music notes (symbolic of the fine arts) are modeled on the capitals of the columns.

Rockhurst Auditorium, used for plays and formal concerts, is now the Monastery dining room/meeting room.

The Chapel of Our Lady Queen of Peace is in the Romanesque style.

CHAPEL OF OUR LADY QUEEN OF PEACE

Located at the center of the esplanade, and set somewhat back of the axial line of Tower Hall and Stanbrook Hall, the Chapel is the focus of the College buildings. Externally it has the following characteristics: cruciform shape, tiled roof, a high sanctuary tower, transept arms projecting a short distance beyond the sides, an attached belfry over the right transept arm, and an elaborate facade. These features mark the Chapel as Romanesque, a style developed by Benedictine abbots of the tenth century, popular with builders of the succeeding period. An example is the Abbey Church, San Miniato al Monte near Florence, built in the year 1013.

Romanesque churches of the eleventh century were long and characteristically low, but, as the surrounding buildings were likely to be lower, their lack of height constituted no defect. The Chapel is 177 feet long. In a building of such length with a high structure at either side, lowness would have been a serious imperfection. This was obviated by assigning the first tier of the building and the space between it and the ground level for a library and making the east cloister walk a means of access to both library and Chapel. At the same time, the long spaces on the exterior of the walls were varied by the cloister walks, the bell tower, the abundant fenestration, and panels of white stone decorated with symbols and inscriptions. One of these panels bears the date on which the cornerstone was laid—July 17, 1937; another, the invocation, *crux sacra sit mihi lux* ("May the holy cross be my light").

Sanctuary and Bell Towers

One may say with truth that all the buildings of the College are tower-crowned, but the west tower of the Chapel, with its outstanding height and central position, is the controlling feature in the skyline. Its lower section, ascending twenty feet above the main roof, is thirty-six feet square at the upper molding. From there it tapers off to a pyramidal dome that gives rise to the tall cone of the spire. Finally, the stem of the spire, rising between two revolute lily leaves—Our Lady's Symbol—flashes over the cap of the cone and terminates in a Roman cross. This shining tip is one-hundred twenty feet above the ground level. And indeed it seems entirely proper that a college of many towers should give pronounced height to one that proclaims its main purpose: that of forming young women to spiritual ideals of mind and heart by means of religious education.

The Chapel bell and campanile can be studied from the Angelus Court, an enclosed garden that derived its name from them. Both of these features have an architectural interest and, therefore, seem to call for some

The bell tower of the Chapel of Our Lady Queen of Peace is capped by "a ship with anchor set and hoisted sails to represent the Church sailing through the storms of persecution to her heavenly port."

The Chapel bell and campanile are best seen from the Angelus Court, between the Chapel and Tower Hall.

description in this chapter. First, the bell: Its median diameter of three feet, with a corresponding weight, does not render its sound either strident or heavy, for the careful proportioning of the metals has resulted in tones that are mellow as well as resonant. Until 1938 the bell hung in the oldest tower of Tower Hall, but when the new Chapel was nearing completion, it was moved to its present home. The campanile is original and symbolically very interesting. Rising from a square base that springs from the junction of the transept and the west cloister walk, it narrows to a cone-shaped dome supported by eight pilasters. Dome and pilasters are encased in antique brass. On the summit is poised a ship with anchor set and hoisted sails to represent the Church sailing through the storms of persecution to her heavenly port.

Scholasticans grow to be pronounced bell lovers. How often have alumnae of the College told with what delight they now hear the sound of church bells, and how they can recall in memory the mellow but insistent tones of "Benedict" announcing the hour for Mass, Benediction, and the Angelus.

CHAPEL FACADE

Stressing the dedication of the Chapel, the east facade is overlaid with Indiana limestone, which is sculptured into figures and Marian iconography. Below the turrets at the upper corners are statues of St. Benedict and St. Scholastica, their shrines displaying the entwined olive branch and briar, flower motifs that devotional literature has always associated with these beloved saints. Beneath the gable cross is the Great East Window, protected by its deep reveal and balcony. Next in order comes a horizontal band of stone, carrying the title of the Chapel done in half relief. A little farther down appears the entrance splay, its double doors recessed six feet behind the threshold and the figure of Our Lady on the *trumeau*. The doors are heavy golden oak, their lower half designed in a concentric sunken panel, their upper half in lights of antique glass.

"Benedict," the bell, was moved from Tower Hall to be reinstalled in the new Chapel in 1938.

Statues of St. Benedict (left) and St. Scholastica (right) atop the facade of the Chapel of Our Lady Queen of Peace

The reveals around the Great East Window and the double portals are surrounded by a huge arch that depicts by means of repeating bosses, seven emblems of the Blessed Virgin. A lily represents the Annunciation; a babe, the Nativity; a censer, the Adoration of the Magi; St. Simeon with scroll, the Presentation in the Temple; a lamb with the paschal banner, the Resurrection of Our Lord; an angel with wings outspread, the Blessed Mother's Assumption into Heaven; a crown, her Coronation as Queen of Angels and of Saints.

The arch splay is also set with bosses that carry symbols of the Blessed Virgin and the three Divine Persons. Reading in order, they are the rod of Aaron budding forth to represent the Virgin Birth; the harp of David to suggest the lineage of our Blessed Lady; the chalice to denote the Lord's Supper; a fish, the Blessed Sacrament; a descending dove to signify the Holy Spirit; a phoenix consumed by fire as it arises to symbolize the Resurrection. A final boss with *triquetra* and the equilateral triangle enclosed within a circle represents the Holy Trinity. Completing this elaborate feature in a manner consistent with the Romanesque style, a series of wide granite steps descends below the portals, crosses the terrace, and, passing through the opening in the balustrade, continues to the sidewalk. The whole design—the statues of the Founders and Our Lady, the reveals, the iconography on the arches, the long esplanade interrupted before the Chapel entrance by two massive blocks of granite, the double flight of steps ascending from the campus—all unite to form an imposing composition. Passengers on ships coming into the Duluth harbor by night tell that the Chapel, illuminated by its floodlights, can be seen by them in clear effect from a distance of some fifty miles.

Many Christian symbols are inscribed on the facade of the Chapel of Our Lady Queen of Peace.

The interior of the original Chapel of Our Lady Queen of Peace was beautiful in the simplicity of its adornment.

CHAPEL INTERIOR

THE NARTHEX

The entrance doors admit to the east cloister walk at its very center, and at either side of the opening, a staircase ascends to the narthex of the Chapel interior. Speaking of this portion of a church, Monsignor Collins in his valuable work, *The Church Edifice and Its Appointments*, says: "The narthex, or the vestibule, is one of the main divisions of the church and consequently should never be wanting. It is recommended where possible to have a door at the terminus of each aisle" (270). In Our Lady Queen of Peace Chapel these requirements are fulfilled. Including the two vestibules, which are

arched off from the main division, the narthex extends the width of the Chapel and has a depth of twelve and one-half feet. All three parts open by double doors to the termini of the aisles.

The narthex adapts itself to many uses, both practical and liturgical: there, the new fire is enkindled on the Vigil of Easter; there, in solemn processions, the celebrant, attended by his cross-bearer and acolytes, stands to chant the official prayers before proceeding up the nave to the altar. At other times, it is a *statio* for students and others coming in numbers to participate in the religious services.

In view of these important uses, it seems fitting that the narthex should be beautiful, and it is. Bare of furnishings except for two holy water fonts of Genevieve Rose marble, its illumination, color, and symbolism combine to make it a place of beauty. The fonts have a certain elegance, which is enhanced by a course of Morocco Red marble in a diamond motif around the bowl [FOR DESCRIPTIONS OF BUILDING RENOVATIONS, SEE APPENDIX B. ED.]. This treatment, which is original and striking, is in harmony with the simplicity of the narthex.

SACRISTIES

At the west end of the Chapel, directly opposite the narthex, are the sacristies. Occupying the space behind the sanctuary, they are entered from the side aisles, which carry back to the end wall. Their generous width and a depth of twenty-five feet give ample space for workroom, storage closets, and accessories. The main sacristy is equipped with a *sacrarium*, a *lavabo*, and a vestment case. Three large windows and four electric lamps supply light. Near the work sacristy, a winding staircase gives access to the passageways around the tower and the galleries, where a fan system is installed to provide the Chapel with means of air conditioning and heating.

THE NAVE

Visitors to the Chapel are invariably impressed by its majesty and simplicity. A sense of its height is felt as the eye catches sight of the stately baldachin and tall

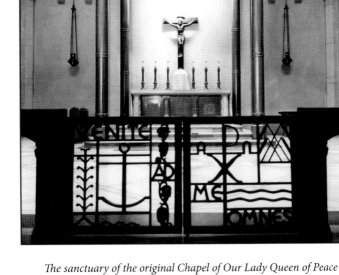

The sanctuary of the original Chapel of Our Lady Queen of Peace

clerestory with wood-trussed roof and pointed rafters, then beholds the great inner tower rising sixty-five feet above the floor level, its aspiring quality emphasized by a flood of light streaming in from its high windows. No less impressive is the sense of its simplicity. The nave extends ninety-seven feet from narthex to communion rail and is forty-four feet wide. Between the aisles, it is clear of all obstruction except for the pews; nothing intervenes to hide the view of the worshipper from the all-important altar. The walls are unmarred by applied ornament; there are no decorative pieces to capture the imagination. Yet there is no monotony, since the stained glass windows cast a pleasing glow, and the Romanesque arch, repeating itself in harmonious rhythm along the aisles, gives sufficient variety.

THE SANCTUARY

The sanctuary (36' x 34') is open at the sides, its only division from the aisles being twelve columns of Winona marble with decorated bell capital and octagonal base. The walls above the columns are relieved by deep recessions, springing behind the capitals of engaged columns at the sanctuary corners. These recessions, encircling the wall from side to side, create a background for two arcades that open into low galleries above the transepts. The arcades are treated in Winona marble and enclosed by hand-wrought iron grilles. Similar recessions on the

The entrance to the library when it was first completed in 1938

back wall, after rising halfway from the floor level to the base of the tower windows, turn inward to form three blind arcades at either side of the baldachin. Medieval piety, reading a symbolic meaning into every item in church architecture, gave a lovely interpretation to these details: the twelve pillars around the altar were twelve apostles commissioned by Christ to spread the Gospel; the trio of arcades was the threefold mission of the Church to teach, to sanctify, to govern; the light from the high windows was the Light of Divine Grace.

Transept Chapels

The transept chapels contain the altars of the Blessed Virgin and St. Joseph. Above the altars, the mural paint-

ings replace the usual statues. Each chapel has a capacity for forty persons, and each has a vestibule with a stairway descending to the west cloister walk or the campus. Since the Chapel is collegiate in purpose, it has no choir stalls, but the west transept could easily sustain a chancel choir, the gallery of the opposite arm being accommodated to organ pipes.

The College Library

In medieval abbeys it was customary to place the library near the church. The College of St. Scholastica has honored the custom. Directly opposite the Chapel entrance, at the middle of the east cloister walk, are three doors encased in maroon leather and adorned by antique pull handles and brass mounts. Small octagons of stained glass inserted in the doors at the ordinary eye level indicate our heritage from books. The designs in the glass suggest symbolically the offerings of the library in science, literature, and the arts. The leather doors open upon a triple stairway descending to a reading room large enough to accommodate 240 readers at one time. Its beamed ceiling, eighteen and one-half feet high, is supported by huge piers near the twenty-four tall windows on the north and south walls and by two rows of octagonal columns near the center. Shelving built along the north and south walls below the windows accommodates five to six thousand reference books. Four smaller rooms, yielding a space of 1,500 square feet, are located below the narthex and the transepts of the Chapel. The first two serve for special reading, the other two as reference rooms for bound and current periodicals. The floors in all of these sections are oak parquetry, noiseless to the tread.

Division between the general reading room and the circulation areas at its west is effected in part by plaster walls wainscoted in oak, in part by oak screens. Ambulatories, starting out from the circulation desk right and left, carry back around the stack room. On their outer sides they give entry to the periodical rooms, the stairways to the Chapel, the offices, storage and service

The colors chosen for the original library created a restful place for research and study.

rooms; on the inner sides, to the stack room. All partitions on both sides of these aisles are composed of steel mullioned glass, lighting up the otherwise dark passageways. Secondary entrances at the north, west, and south of the stack room also communicate with the ambulatories. Hence, the library is accessible from every section of the campus.

Three doors west of the circulation area admit to the stack room. It is forty-two feet square and eighteen and a half feet high. At present, it has shelving for 40,000 volumes, but this number can be doubled by a second tier of shelves. Lighting is taken care of by six tall windows and by electric switches; heating and ventilation, by an electric fan system.

Lucille Fargo, in a standard work, states that libraries are places "where young people should cultivate, along with learning, a sense of the aesthetic" (22), and St. Thomas Aquinas tells us that the objective qualities of the aesthetic are integrity or wholeness, harmony of proportion, and splendor of form (I, 39, a8). These

Victory Hall, built in 1945 and enlarged in 1950, was the home of student nurses from The College of St. Scholastica for many years.

Our Lady of Victory

conditions, expressed in the ordering of space, are spoken more emphatically in symbolism and color. In all reading rooms the paneling and wainscoting are of golden oak. Sometimes these are adorned with the carved acanthus; at other times, with the linen-fold. The library tables are polychromed in green and burnt sienna. Stained glass and statues in their niches give a touch of brilliance. The large oaken panel behind the circulation desk is carved in seven concentric diamonds to signify the unity of knowledge. The hoods on the wall tables are fluted at the bottom and finished in the egg and dart motif. Very happily, these hoods conform in height with the tops of the bookcases on the north and south walls, so that all around the main reading room, paintings, artistic prints, and other *objects d'art* may be placed there on exhibition.

VICTORY HALL

The last member of the group of College buildings is Victory Hall, completed in 1950. As previously mentioned in the history, it is a residence for the nurses who receive their clinical training in St. Mary's Hospital and their liberal arts courses on the main campus. Being located on Fourth Avenue East and Fourth Street, in close proximity to the hospital, it resembles that building in its external characteristics. It is built of reddish brick, is rectangular in shape, and is six stories high. The building is modern and functional in construction rather than deliberately aesthetic. However, its situation on the corner of the block, its length (220 feet), and especially its formal terrace and attractive entrance make it an impressive structure. Very fittingly, a statue of Our Lady of Victory stands above the portico. The figure is carved from an unusually fine piece of Bedford stone and is an original interpretation of its subject. [FOR CURRENT LOCATION OF THE STATUE, SEE APPENDIX A, ED.] Interiorly the building is well planned and modernly equipped to be an ideal home for nurses. There are in it rooms for 160 persons, along with social and recreational quarters, an administrative unit, and a library. From the upper story windows the view of Duluth and its cascading hills is very beautiful.

VII: Appointments of the Chapel

Every care was taken to insure that the altar appointments of the Chapel of Our Lady Queen of Peace would be in conformity with the requirements of *Canon Law* and the *Acts of the Congregation of the Sacraments* while satisfying the architectural implications of the building.

They are therefore liturgical rather than elaborate, and their decorative elements are symbolic. In the Christian church every piece is a symbol in itself. Its ornament is but a reminder of its spiritual significance, an outward sign of the inner truth it represents. Since the architecture of the Chapel is Early Christian and Romanesque, the ornament is derived from the religious art expression of the two periods.

ALTARS AND ALTAR APPOINTMENTS

HIGH ALTAR

The high altar is freestanding and is twelve feet long, four feet deep, and about thirty-nine inches high. It is made from Kesota [WINONA, ED.] marble, a stone especially fitting for an altar on account of its great durability and the mellow beauty of its gold and gray tones. Its two parts—the *mensa* or altar table, and the columns—were constructed from a single piece of marble and were cemented together before the altar was placed on the *praedella*. The support below the *mensa* extends the full width of the altar table and is sculpted at the ends into columns, or stipes, as they are technically called. Between these is a wide panel recessed

The high altar in the original Chapel of Our Lady Queen of Peace

twenty inches from the edge of the *mensa* and divided into three parts. The entire frontal is richly carved with Early Christian symbolism: on the *mensa*, incised in deep lettering, is the Trisagion, "*Sanctus, Sanctus, Sanctus*"; on the columns are carved quatrefoils, diamonds, and grapes, early symbols respectively of the Redemption, the Holy Trinity, and the Blessed Sacrament; on the outer divisions of the central panel are the Alpha and Omega, signifying God, the Beginning and End of all things; and on the center panel, the Chi Rho, Christ, Whom the altar represents.

This altar was solemnly consecrated by His Excellency, the Most Reverend Thomas A. Welch, attended by several members of the clergy, on August 15, 1938. In the beautiful ceremony of consecration, the relics of St. Vincent and St. Agatha, martyrs of the early Church, were deposited in the sepulcher, and the altar was dedicated to Our Lady Queen of Peace.

An angel from the original baldachin in the Chapel of Our Lady Queen of Peace

TABERNACLE
Since the high altar in the Chapel is a "reserved altar"—that is, one in which the Sacred Host is kept—it has a tabernacle firmly attached near the center of the *mensa*. The tabernacle stands free on all sides in order that the veils may be conveniently changed to agree with the official color of the day. In conformity with liturgical requirements, it has a self-locking door with key opening and two separate steel linings, making an interior steel chamber. Inside of this chamber is still another lining of precious cedar wood. The floor of the tabernacle is covered with a linen corporal. All of these precautions are in conformity with the regulations laid down by the *Acts of the Congregation of the Sacraments* in order to safeguard the Sacred Species and protect it against dampness or decay.

The outer wall, rendered in antique cast bronze, is a dome-shaped structure fifty inches high, thirty-eight inches in diameter, surmounted by an eight-pointed crown. The surface of the dome is divided into eight panels, all delicately carved and chased in symbols of the Holy Eucharist and the Holy Sacrifice of the Mass.

BALDACHIN
The baldachin over the high altar is made of soft beech wood, lacquered in antique gold and adorned with angels, crosses, and floral motifs. Standing within

the axis of the great tower, with which it is in scale, it rises gracefully to a height of thirty-three feet above the floor level. Though a unit, it may be considered in three parts: the piers, the canopy, and the cupola at its summit. All of these parts are richly carved in symbols chosen from Early Christian and Romanesque art. On the piers are balls and crosses in high relief; on the lowest molding of the canopy is a wide floral band of grapes and chevrons; above this runs a panel in balustrade effect; and, at top, a molding composed of rose petals. The floral motifs are polychromed in rose and light green, while the

The interior of the Chapel of Our Lady Queen of Peace

guardian angels that form the cornices of the canopy are in Roman gold. Very interesting is the cupola. In form it is a coronet resting on twelve graceful pillars and is topped by a rayed cross with adoring seraphim kneeling at its foot. [For descriptions of building renovations, see Appendix B. Ed.].

Side Altars

Resembling the high altar in material and design, the side altars are in every sense liturgical. They are made from Kesota [Winona, Ed.] marble and follow the Church's regulations as to size and placement. Throughout the year, Holy Mass is offered daily at the high altar and at the altar in the Lady Chapel; during the vacation months, the three altars are often used simultaneously. On Holy Thursday and Good Friday morning, the St. Joseph Chapel is a reserved chapel, where the Blessed Sacrament is placed in a repository urn over the altar of repose. By harmonizing the frames of the murals over the side altars with the baldachin, a pleasing balance between the three units has been achieved.

Altar Appointments

All the altar appointments are in accord with the Church's regulations. Ten candlesticks, six high and four low, and the Bishop's candlestick (fixed behind the tabernacle) were carved from black walnut, making for the high altar a single set with the altar crucifix. The tall candlesticks reach to the base of the crucifix. An interesting combination of the altar cards was invented by Monsignor George Gallik when he was chaplain of the College. The three cards are brought together within a frame of handwrought bronze, convexly shaped so as to fit around the tabernacle and revolve easily when its door is opened.

The crucifix above the altar was created in rough-hewn oak and American black walnut by Harry Eversfield Donohue.

THE ALTAR CRUCIFIX

Above the high altar hangs a crucifix with a *corpus* three-quarter life size. The cross is rough-hewn oak; the figure is American black walnut, and is an original conception of the artist, Harry Eversfield Donohue of Ossining, New York. It represents the Redeemer of the World at the moment when He utters the fourth word

from the cross: "My God, My God! Why hast Thou forsaken Me?" (Matthew 27:46) This poignant moment is depicted with power and with the correct balance between styles tending neither to extreme realism nor to excessive symbolism. Mr. Donohue made the statue soon after the death of his young wife, lovely and beloved, who left three children motherless. In a letter to the writer dated December 12, 1948, he described his conception in these words: "Feeling as I do, that in the lesson the fourth word of Christ on the cross brings lies the road to salvation, I desire with all my heart that those who look upon this crucifix may see what I so keenly realized when I made it: only by yielding to the will and love of God can man be saved." Those who gaze upon this beautiful crucifix attest by word and look how well the artist succeeded in expressing his inspiration. [FOR DESCRIPTIONS OF BUILDING RENOVATIONS, SEE APPENDIX B. ED.].

SANCTUARY APPOINTMENTS

FURNITURE

The sanctuary furniture—credence table, *sedila*, *prieudieux*, chairs, and also a sacerdotal throne used on occasions when the Most Reverend Bishop pontificates or is present at the services—is constructed of quarter-sawn oak, in the Byzantine mode and polychromed to agree in color with the communion rail. Their decorative motifs, carved in high relief, fall naturally into patterns in which crosses, stars, octagons, circles, rosettes, trefoils, and acanthus leaves are gracefully combined.

COMMUNION RAIL

This delicately rendered piece is made from select oak, exquisitely polished and polychromed in mingled tones of green, gray, and yellow. At the point where the railing joins the pulpit, the terminals of the uprights take the form of a cathedral or a crown, both of which are symbols of the Church. They are Early Christian in design, as are the other carvings on the rail, especially the Ichthus and the Dove. The gateway is of wrought iron and bronze at the center of the railing. [FOR DESCRIPTIONS OF BUILDING RENOVATIONS, SEE APPENDIX B. ED.]

PULPIT

Although a pulpit is not strictly prescribed for a collegiate chapel, it is recommended that every church in which sermons are regularly given have a pulpit, so located that the preacher can see his audience and can be seen by them. In connection with the sermons, our pulpit fills a most important role, since eight to ten retreats and many sermons are yearly given in the Chapel. It is placed at the end of the Communion rail on the Gospel side. Finished in the same manner as the railing, its attractive features are its alternating sunken and raised paneling, its carved reading stand, and a course of four-pointed stars carved below the upper molding. Apparently its dimensions, a little more than six feet above the floor and four feet across, are correct, for many clergymen who have spoken from it have pronounced it a convenient rostrum.

This picture of Our Lady Chapel shows the beautifully carved furniture in the sanctuary.

Sister Yvonne Campbell, sacristan, prepares the vessels for the altar in the sacristy.

ALTAR VESTMENTS, VEILS, AND VESTMENT CASE

Several complete sets of vestments and altar veils are provided in each of the liturgical colors—white, green, red, violet, black. Rose vestments and veil are worn on *Gaudete* and *Laetare* Sundays. All the vestments are in ample mode, and a number of sets are adorned with hand embroidery.

A handsome vestment case of quarter-sawn oak stands against the wall of the sacristy directly behind the altar. It is ten feet wide and contains eighteen drawers below the table for the storage of vestments and twelve compartments above for the safekeeping of other altar furnishings. The case shows a considerable amount of artistic work. Its end panels, doors, and oaken handles are in the linen-fold design, a popular motif of Romanesque Art.

The stations in the Chapel were carved from American black walnut by Harry Eversfield Donohue of Ossining, New York, who carved the altar crucifix. As original creations, they differ in several ways from the stations ordinarily seen in churches. To begin with, they are not marked by numbers. Before the eighteenth century the number of stations varied. At one time seven stopping places were chosen; at another, twenty-one. Today, the matter is decided for us by the Church. There are fourteen, but the pilgrim who meditates upon them is well aware that Christ's *Via Crucis* was a continuous way. Secondly, our stations are relatively small (24" by 16"). Largeness is neither necessary nor desirable. Again, our stations picture no elaborate scenes with soldiers in their armor or bearded rabbis carrying scrolls. Christ is the essential figure; other participants come in only where the idea cannot be made clear by showing Him alone. Lastly, the story is told by means of actions and by the engraved Latin texts, which were selected from the Psalms, the hymns of Holy Week, and from passages in Holy Scripture. [THE STATIONS OF THE CROSS WERE CANONICALLY ERECTED BY THE RIGHT REVEREND MICHAEL BOLAND, SEPTEMBER 17, 1938. ED.]

Christ's Passion is for us a concrete meditation on the necessity of patient suffering as a means of obtaining an eternal reward. "Take up thy cross and follow Me" (Matthew 17:24), He said; and again, "I am the Way" (John 14:6). The texts appended to the first and last stations form a prelude and a conclusion to the meditative theme. They are in Latin but are no less effective in translation. Willing acceptance of the Cross is the keynote of the opening text: "Looking on Jesus, the author and finisher of faith, Who having joy set before Him endured the cross, despising its shame" (Hebrews 12:2). In the fourteenth station, we hear the note of triumph that follows the patient bearing of the Cross to the end: "I am the Resurrection and the Life. He that believeth in Me, although he be dead, shall live; and everyone that liveth and believeth in Me, shall not die forever" (John 11:25).

The captions under the images of the stations on the next few pages include the accepted name of the station and the text that forms the theme of each meditation.

I. JESUS IS CONDEMNED TO DEATH

Reus est mortis:
He is guilty of death (Matthew 26:66).

In the first station, Jesus accepts with equanimity the judgment of death, for He knows that by dying He can redeem the Kingdom of Heaven for those whom He loves.

II. Jesus Takes Up His Cross

Ave crux spes unica: Hail,
Cross, our only hope (*Vexilla Regis*).

Jesus steps forward and eagerly
embraces the cross,
the bitter prelude to glory.

III. Jesus Falls the First Time Beneath the Cross

Timor et tremor venerunt super me:
Fear and trembling came over me (Psalms 55:5).

The ascent to Calvary, carrying the burden of our sins,
crushes Our Redeemer's human nature to the earth,
but His divinity urges Him on.

IV. Jesus Meets His Afflicted Mother

Fac me tecum plangere:
Let me share Thy grief with Thee (*Stabat Mater Prodeunt*).

The depth of Mary's sorrow and her Son's compassion
for her are too great for human understanding.
The Mother of Jesus is represented as asking
Jesus to let her share His agony.

V. Simon of Cyrene Is Forced to Assist Jesus

Tolle crucem sequere Me:
Take up thy cross and follow Me (Luke 9:23).

Christ allows the reluctant Simon to share His burden
and His glory. Simon represents our poor, weak selves,
carrying the cross by compulsion at first; later
bearing it joyfully in union with Christ.

VI. Veronica Wipes the Face of Jesus

Peccata nostra diluas per Veronica lacrimas:
By the tears of Veronica may our sins be blotted out.

Christ allows Veronica to receive in her
veil the impression of His face that
she may show it to the world.

VII. Jesus Falls the Second Time

Multiplicata est super Me iniquitas superborum: The iniquities of the
proud increased against me (Psalms 118:69).

The infinity of pride and selfishness that will fill the world
despite His sacrifice lashes Jesus with stripes of
anguish so that He falls again.

VIII. Jesus Meets the Women of Jerusalem

Filiae Jerusalem flete super filios: Daughters of Jerusalem,
weep over your children (Luke 23:28).

Christ warns the Jewish mothers of the anguish
that will be the heritage of their children
and their children's children.

IX. Jesus Falls the Third Time

Cecidi in terram clamans, Domine Deus!:
He fell upon the earth crying, "O Lord, my God!"

Christ's agony as He nears the end of His journey
is almost intolerable, causing Him to fall again
and to cry out to His Father.

X. Jesus Is Stripped of His Garments

Induit Eum cominus vestimentis salutis: The Lord has clothed
Him with the garment of our salvation (Isaiah 61:10).

Before the final holocaust, Jesus gives up even the garment
that covers His bruised Body, that He may meet
His Father utterly destitute.

XI. Jesus Is Nailed to the Cross

Quae sunt plagae istae in medio manum?: What are these wounds in
the midst of My hands? (Zechariah 13:6).

Jesus opens His hands
to receive the wounds
that would heal mankind.

XII. Jesus Dies on the Cross

Regnavit a lingo Deus:
God reigned from the tree of the cross (*Vexilla Regis Prodeunt*).

With arms uplifted to His Father
and outstretched to mankind,
Jesus dies on the cross,
the symbol of Infinite Love for all time.

XIII. Jesus Is Taken Down from the Cross

Salveta Christi Vulnera: Save us, wounds of Christ.

Joseph of Arimathea went to Pilate and asked for the
body of Jesus, and Pilate gave permission. Then Joseph and
Nicodemus took the body of Jesus down from the cross
(John 19: 38-40). Waiting there was His Mother who took
His bruised body into her arms and clasped it to her breast.

XIV. Jesus Is Laid in the Sepulchre

Memento Mei Domine in regno Tuo:
Remember Me Lord, in Thy kingdom (Luke 23:42).

The body of Jesus is laid in the new tomb,
symbolic of the new meaning of death,
while his spirit descends into limbo
to open the gates of heaven for the good thief
and all those who had loved God on earth.

[Station XIII is omitted from Sister Agnes Somers' edition. The editor, Sister Joan Braun, included XIII.
For the current location of the Stations, see Appendix A. Ed.]

VIII. Stained Glass Windows

Ever since the middle of the twelfth century when stained glass was introduced into the West, it has been a means of conveying lessons of piety to the faithful. Scenes and characters of the Old Testament, the miracles and parables of Christ, the mysteries of the rosary, and the role of the Blessed Virgin under her many titles have been powerfully impressed through the use of color. Sometimes the subject is presented individually, sometimes in a series that develops a religious theme. But whatever the mode of presentation, the main object is always to teach and to inspire devotion in the churchgoer. To preach sermons that will reach the heart through the eyes is the proper tradition of ecclesiastical glass painting. [FOR CURRENT LOCATION OF THE STAINED GLASS WINDOWS, SEE APPENDIX B, DESCRIPTIONS OF BUILDING RENOVATIONS. ED.]

WINDOWS OF THE CHAPEL

Following this tradition, the windows in the Chapel of Our Lady Queen of Peace develop a theme in keeping with the dedication of the building to our Blessed Mother. The Great East Window of the facade displays, in majestic figure, Our Lady Queen of Peace. Around her are figures and symbols representing persons and institutions that have been harbingers of peace to humanity. The seventeen major windows of the aisles enter into the development of the peace theme by presenting seventeen women whose holy lives and great achievements made them instruments of peace in the world of their day. These saintly women are exemplars for the young women students of the College because they show by their virtues and deeds the manner in which women can help bring about an ideal social order—a world of justice, charity, and peace. Each one typifies a form of Christian activity through which women can accomplish their mission. Mary, their queen and leader, encourages their beneficence and makes them sharers in her worldwide apostolate of peace. While this theme has the note of universality that would render its message appropriate in any period or any condition of society, its immediacy to our present needs gives it a vital, contemporary interest.

Altogether the Chapel has eighty-three windows, designed from imported colored glass leaded into figures and symbols appropriate to the central theme. Two motifs are cleverly combined in the background glass: the Romanesque quatrefoil and the Roman cross. And since glass, better than any

Some of the original stained glass windows can be seen today in the Eucharistic Chapel, behind the main altar of the current Chapel.

other medium, can express the glory of color, each subject has its place in a well-planned rotation of the chromatic scale with its complete cycle of shades and tints. Especially interesting in respect to color display is the Great East Window; next in interest are the figure windows in the side aisles. The glass around the sanctuary and in the clerestory has no figures, but it emphasizes the background pattern and helps to diffuse light and especially color. The eighteen amber windows illuminate the great tower; the two windows at the west end of the aisles are brilliant in mandarin orange with an offset of nile green; the windows in the transepts interlace the cross and quatrefoil in glass of turquoise blue. The clerestory windows, two of which rise above each of the bays, repeat the colors in the glass below in a range of lighter, more vibrant shades.

Of the twelve windows in the narthex, the color that continues Our Lady's mantle from the gallery above is predominantly ruby with an offset of black. The smaller windows are rose, green, and gray.

The Great East Window has a height of seventeen feet at its center and a width of twelve feet at its base; the aisle windows have a height of nine feet and a width of three feet. The other windows vary in size according to their setting and purpose.

Saints in the Aisle Windows

[In the following text Sister Agnes Somers writes about each window. The following photos of the windows do not include the casement sections she describes. [For descriptions of building renovations, see Appendix B. Ed.]

St. Catherine of Alexandria

St. Anne

St. Catherine of Alexandria: "True Philosophy"

With her right hand she points to a scroll on which is engraved the word "*Philosophia*," signifying her wisdom in meeting the arguments of the philosophers who sought to dissuade her from Christian truth. Her left hand grasps the cross, symbol of her faith. A lily in the right-hand casement recalls the title an ancient Greek biographer gave her, namely, "The Ever Pure." The right-hand casement shows also the wheel that was constructed at the command of the emperor to accomplish her martyrdom. Near the top of the main panel, at the left, we see a symbol of the Three Divine Persons: the hand through the clouds is the symbol for God the Father; the Chi Rho, for God the Son; the dove, for the Holy Spirit. St. Catherine was devoted to the Holy Trinity.

St. Anne: "Motherhood"

St. Anne gave us Mary, and Mary, in turn, gave us Christ. Her role of motherhood is indicated throughout the window beginning at the right casement, continuing to the left, and ascending to the top of the main panel by the position of the figures, which signify a genealogy. This same idea is further stressed by a pomegranate vine, symbol of Motherhood, at the right side of the main panel. Mary, Mother of the Divine Child, is the link between Judaism and Christianity. Again, the relation is brought out by symbols: the Ark of the Covenant in the casement at our right, the Star of David in the casement at our left. The New Law is indicated by a lily for Mary; a cross and a crown for Christ, king of the New Dispensation.

St. Elizabeth of Hungary

Blessed Kateri Tekakwitha

St. Elizabeth of Hungary: "Christian Social Service"

St. Elizabeth's regal dignity is portrayed by the crown that she wears over her veil. Her great love for her husband is expressed by the intertwined rings near her right hand. Even as a queen, she spent much of her time ministering to the poor, a fact signified by the bread turned to roses, as seen in the left casement. After the death of her husband, she became a Franciscan tertiary in order that she might more worthily serve the needy. The Franciscan symbol of the crossed arms of St. Francis and Christ in the right casement denotes that, like St. Francis, she became poor in imitation of Christ.

Blessed Kateri Tekakwitha: "Willing Sacrifice"

Blessed Kateri is shown standing before a large cross, an attitude that reminds us of her faith and fortitude. In her adherence to the cross of Christ, she exemplifies patience, courage, and love of penance. She was noted also for her purity; she is called the "Lily of the Mohawks." The tepee at her feet and the Indian blankets that envelop her are introduced to indicate her race. The plant and animal forms in the background stress her native environment. A nocturnal owl, a mythical thunderbird, and a creeping turtle are significant of the animal spirit that pervades Indian mythology. Wild roses and daisies are scattered here and there. The Jesuit symbol in the casement suggests her conversion by the American Jesuit missionaries.

Mother Cabrini

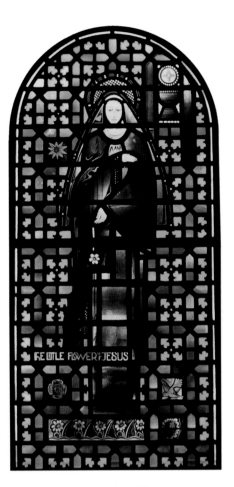

St. Therese of the Child Jesus

MOTHER CABRINI:
"MISSIONARY ZEAL"

The phase of Mother Cabrini's activities stressed in this window is her work, conducted at the request of the Holy Father, for Italian emigrants and their children. The figure in the main panel represents her in the act of dividing her cloak to clothe two orphans. The map of North and South America on that part of the globe turned toward us denotes that these countries were the scene of her missionary zeal.

The Chi Rho and the cross proclaim the objective of all her labor, while the dome of St. Peter's in the casement window signifies her obedience to the Holy See.

THE LITTLE FLOWER:
"THE GREATNESS OF LITTLENESS"

St. Therese of the Child Jesus, the Little Flower as she is lovingly called, is great in her boundless desire to help everyone in the world who needs help. In life, she longed to be a missionary and a martyr, to give herself for the sanctification of souls, especially for the sanctification of the priesthood. Before her death, she promised to spend her heaven doing good, to "let fall a shower of roses," as she phrased it. In this window, she is shown holding a flower in her left hand. Other flowers, especially roses, are scattered in the background. Her zeal for the priestly ministry is betokened by the host and the chalice at the upper right of the main panel. Her signature "I C Theresa X C," (Jesus conquers all) evinces her total dependence on the power and goodness of God.

St. Cecilia

St. Martha

St. Cecilia:
"Conversion to the Faith of Christ"

This lovely saint is seen with her husband, Valerianus, and his brother, Tiburtius, both of whom she converted to Christianity. Above her head is a cross; below her, a design of the classical fret, defining her Roman lineage as well as the period in which she lived and died. St. Cecilia is represented in poetry and art as the patroness of music. An insert displays a row of organ pipes. However, the organ is a minor motif in this presentation. More important are the crown and the palm in the left casement, symbolic of the rewards of her martyrdom.

St. Martha:
"Devotion to Household Duties"

St. Martha is shown kneeling before Our Lord, holding in her hands a tray containing bread and fish. Christ blesses her and at the same time blesses the food. Near her feet is a spindle, for Martha is "a valiant woman who wrought wool and flax by the counsel of her hands" (Proverbs 31:13). The ring and keys in the left casement declare St. Martha's careful attention to her housekeeping. A cross in the other casement denotes that she glorified these homely duties by dedicating them to Christ.

St. Agnes

St. Scholastica

St. Agnes:
"Love of Christ"

St. Agnes stands, a youthful figure, proclaiming her love for Christ by her chosen motto *"Amo Christum,"* to which she points with her left hand. This motto, which is at the upper left of the panel, forms the crossed arms of the Chi Rho. In her right hand, the Saint holds a lily, significant of her purity. An insert at the lower left of the main panel introduces a lamb, suggesting a custom still followed in the Church of St. Agnes in Rome, that of blessing there every year the lambs from whose wool the pallia of newly chosen bishops are made. Flames of fire and a sword in the left casement, a crown and a palm branch in the right, denote the manner of St. Agnes' martyrdom, which occurred in A.D. 304 under the Roman Emperor Diocletian.

St. Scholastica: "Christian Education"

St. Scholastica was the sister of St. Benedict, founder of the Benedictine Order. In the window, an abbatial staff indicates her dignity as Abbess. Moreover, she is the patroness of the Benedictine schools conducted by women and the first in a long line of teaching nuns. The upper part of the main panel displays a *Rule of St. Benedict* to indicate that she was directed by the wise counsels of her saintly brother. Two nuns at the lower part of the panel are reciting the *Opus Dei*, or the Divine Office. The casement windows show two aspirants of the Order engaged in the humble task of sweeping the floor. St. Benedict dignified manual work—which the ancients considered to be fit only for slaves—by requiring that his monks should engage in the labor of the hands. St. Scholastica made a like requirement for her nuns.

St. Gertrude

St. Hildegarde

St. Gertrude:
"The Apostolate of the Written Word"

St. Gertrude helped to clarify the Word of God and to bring others to greater perfection by her writings. This is signified by the Greek word *Logos*, "the Word of God," which is inscribed in the upper part of the large panel. The saint holds on her left arm the *Legatus Divinae Pietatis* in four volumes, her principal work; lower down in the main panel is her best-known book, *Exercitia Spiritualia*. St. Gertrude's devotion to the Sacred Heart is indicated by the figure of Our Lord; a monstrance opposite the figure proclaims her devotion to the Blessed Sacrament. An insert with the symbolic ink and quill refers to her avocation as a writer.

St. Hildegarde:
"Scientific Care of the Sick"

The saint stands in the center of the main panel at the bedside of a patient to whom another is administering medicine. She holds on her arm the *Scivias*, her first and greatest book. Another work in several volumes, entitled *Curae et Causae* because it explains the ailments of the human body and their causes and treatment, is suggested by inserts at the base of the main panel. The caduceus, a symbol of the medical profession, is seen at the left of the saint. In the casements are two figures: the one standing in an attitude of thought represents St. Hildegarde; the other sitting near her and writing is her scribe.

St. Genevieve

St. Rose of Lima

St. Genevieve: "Catholic Action"

The activities attributed to this saint are many. When only twelve years of age, she was singled out for a career of sanctity by St. Germaine, the great patron saint of France, who is shown in the main panel, blessing her and placing a medal around her neck. Although she lived in the fifth century at a turbulent time, she was entrusted by the Bishop of Paris with a work that today approximates that of Regional Prefect of Our Lady's Sodality. She gathered around her the young women of Paris, instructed them in religion, and led them in its practice. St. Genevieve is pictured in art as a shepherdess. While there seems to be no foundation for the story that Genevieve engaged in prayer while her flocks grazed quietly on the mountainside, it is at least a pretty legend, repeated in the windows by the three lambs, which rest tranquilly in the casements. History attests that on two occasions Genevieve saved the city of Paris, of which she has always been considered the Patroness.

St. Rose of Lima: "Confidence in Our Lady"

St. Rose of Lima is patroness of the Americas, hence the map of the Western Hemisphere in one of the lower casements. Her intense devotion to Our Lady is evidenced by an insert of the Madonna and Child near the top of the window, her virginity by the lily, her love of Christ by the rose. It is said that in childhood she was given the name "Rose" because her countenance was transfigured by a beauty like that of Our Lady, the "Mystical Rose." All biographies of St. Rose emphasize her spirit of penance. The inset of the Chalice and Host tell of her devotion to the Blessed Sacrament.

St. Catherine of Siena

St. Brigid of Ireland

St. Catherine of Siena:
"Love of the Church"

Skilled in the spiritual direction of souls, successful in her efforts to restore the Holy Father to his traditional see, able to live for long periods without food other than the Holy Eucharist, St. Catherine is probably the most remarkable woman in history. A band of light in triangular frets is symbolic of the wise direction she gave those men and women who came to her for spiritual guidance. The tiara and crossed keys point to her untiring work for the Church; the large ciborium with the grapevine and grapes recall the miraculous manner in which she was sustained solely by the Body and Blood of Christ. Catherine received the stigmata, although by her own wish the marks did not show. In the window, the raised hands of the figure are meant to suggest this singular honor.

St. Brigid of Ireland:
"Hospitality"

St. Brigid is represented with outstretched arms embracing two persons in need of counsel or shelter: one intended to denote the rich, the other the poor. They kneel at her feet in an attitude of confidence. Above and to the right of the saint is the Church of the Oak. Brigid was a builder of many churches. She was also a foundress of schools. Her devotion to learning is suggested by the famous *Book of Kildare*, shown below the two figures. A scrip in the left casement stands for the pilgrims who came to the Well of St. Brigid to bathe in its healing waters; the shamrock on the right casement recalls her friendship with St. Patrick.

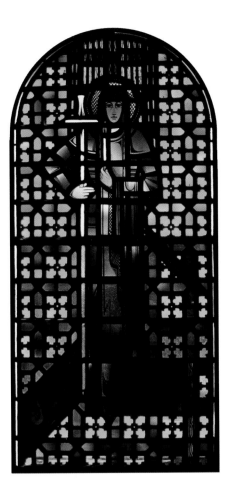

St. Joan of Arc

St. Joan of Arc: "Patriotism"

This lovely saint is presented in the hooded cloak and other caparison of a soldier. Her right hand holds a shining spear. Above her head eight descending waves of light indicate the Heavenly Voices that announced her mission to save France from English aggression. Near her feet at her right are the fires of her martyrdom; at her left the crown and insignia of her native land. The stained glass window of Reims Cathedral in the casement to our left and the fleur-de-lis she carries are symbolic of the religious ideals of French art in the age of faith.

Great East Window

Our Lady Queen of Peace

Our Lady rises from the outspreading Root of Jesse, the symbol of her mission as the new Eve. This mystical vine first grows to a pomegranate, then to the lily, whence it spreads outward to include the panels at the sides. The Christogram is above Mary's head. Angels at either side hold a glowing mantle, which forms the background of the window and then reaches down to include the windows of the narthex. Thus, in its generous spread, the mantle signifies Our Lady's solicitude for the whole world. The theme of the window is peace: peace among the nations, peace in the individual soul, and peace in the social order. The figures in the window are symbolic of the various channels through which peace is obtained. Conversion to Christianity has brought peace to all races. This is signified by the figures of four missionaries: St. Peter Claver, St. Francis Xavier, [St. Patrick, and St. Isaac Jogues. Ed]. In each case, a figure representing the race evangelized is introduced below the arms of the missionary. But peace thus gained is unhappily lost through man's greed and ambition. It must be restored by constant emphasis on the teachings of Christ. Two peace popes, Benedict XV and Pius XI, kneel beside Our Lady in the central panel, one at each end of the rainbow of peace. Insistent in their protests against the evils that produced the two tragic wars of the present century, they implore Mary, Queen of Peace, to give efficacy to their pleadings for a return of peace among nations.

But individuals and social groups must also have peace. It comes to the individual soul through the grace of the sacraments: the peace of God's kingdom on earth through Baptism; the peace of the heavenly kingdom through Extreme Unction. The traditional symbols of these two sacraments are in the outer panels while "the tranquility of order" through law and government are indicated by the symbol of jurisprudence at the foot of the central panel. The inner corner of the left panel

The Great East Window of the Chapel of Our Lady Queen of Peace

displays a cathedral; the opposite panel, a college. They signify that through religion and education social peace is made more secure. Finally, at the bottom of the central panel, the characteristic emblems of capital and labor are shown as an indication that these two opposing forces should find in Our Lady a peaceful solution of their economic difficulties.

The windows were designed and made by Mr. Emil Frei, stained glass artist of St. Louis, Missouri, after he had worked out the general plan and symbolism.

IX. The Benedictines in the Liturgical Revival

Throughout the Middle Ages church music dominated secular music; hence, most of the secular melodies were based on the Gregorian modes. In the second phase of Humanism, prevalent during the fifteenth century, this order was partially reversed. Then, with the birth of opera in 1594, the

song forms of the theater made their way into the churches, and the organ, used as a background for liturgical singing since the Carolingian era, was supplemented by orchestral instruments.

The Church was aware of these abuses and made efforts to correct them. In the sixteenth century the Council of Trent rejected most of the liturgical changes made by the Humanists. Also from time to time during the succeeding centuries, norms were laid down for the guidance of pastors and choir directors. But outside of the Roman churches and some of the great religious houses, the norms were poorly observed. As a consequence, the decadence continued and at last became so widespread that in 1903 Pius X, newly elected pope, began a vigorous world-wide reform.

Soon after his election to the papacy, he commissioned the monks of Solesmes to make an exhaustive study of the early church music. A year later he gave their work the highest possible recognition when, in his *Motu Proprio*, he commissioned the French Benedictine Congregation and the Monastery of Solesmes to prepare an official Vatican edition of the Church's chant. At the same time he asked that "in all seminaries and religious institutes the Gregorian chant be diligently and zealously pursued and that the old *Schola Cantorum* be restored, at least in the principal churches" (Pius X).

This request of the Holy Father gave new impetus to the Benedictines to promote their traditional plainsong. Solesmes revised the *Liber Usualis* and, along with other great abbeys, established courses in liturgical music for clergy and laity. So many of the abbeys, both in Europe and America, have now acquired excellence in the art that it is difficult to say which are outstanding. Among American houses, perhaps the most liturgical minded at the present time are Conception Abbey in Missouri, St. John's Abbey in Minnesota, and St. Meinrad's Abbey in Indiana, which maintain high standards both in chant and organ.

DEVELOPMENT OF THE LITURGY AT ST. SCHOLASTICA

A year after the promulgation of the decree of 1904, Mother Scholastica invited Professor John Singenberger, a noted authority on church music, to conduct a course at Sacred Heart Institute. For seven or eight

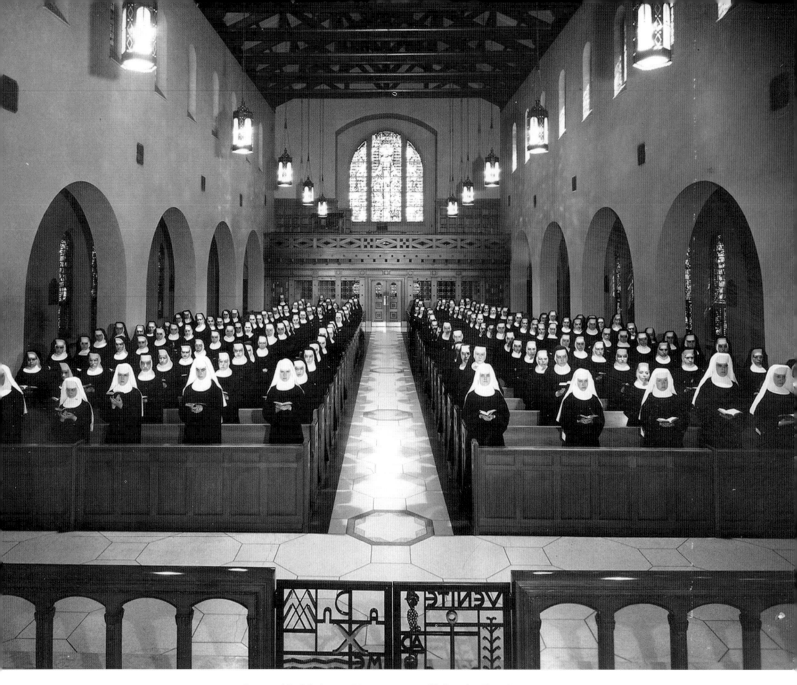

Sisters of St. Scholastica Monastery assembled in the Chapel in 1946.

hours daily during the summer session, he taught sacred polyphony and organ and gave some instruction on the rubrics and Gregorian chant. Later in the year, the choir directress and the organist of the Institute went to study Gregorian music under Dom Gregory Huegle, OSB, of Conception Abbey, Missouri.

Father Gregory, trained in music by the monks of Einsiedeln and by the famous liturgist Dom Andre Moquereau of Solesmes, was a profound scholar of the chant and one of the great teachers of his time. He inspired the Sisters with his zeal for Gregorian music; they, on their return, communicated some spark of that same enthusiasm to the Community. It was introduced at Sacred Heart Institute and from there was continued at the College, which henceforth made it one of its mediums of "sung prayer." Professor Singenberger came again in 1910 to give another summer of sacred music. This time he put more emphasis on the Gregorian. From its very beginning in 1912, the College profited by these instructions.

In 1923 the Sisters replaced the Little Office of the Blessed Virgin with the Divine Office, and the students learned something of the history of this ancient yet ever modern prayer. These

The Skyline Singers, the College choir, about 1938

that year, but its teacher [SISTER MARTINA HUGHES, ED.], still active in the College, has vividly preserved its memory. She says: "It was assigned to me, and although I felt quite unprepared to teach it and accepted the assignment with trepidation, I found the course enthralling; the students were an eager group, and the Missal, in which Mother Church reveals her life of grace, was a constant revelation to us all." From that time forth, liturgy was on the yearly schedule, and the use of the Missal became general. That year the *Missa Recitata* was begun. Since Chapel space was limited, the

were, of course, but partial glimpses of the liturgy; a larger view began to open in November 1926, when St. John's Abbey published its first issue of *Orate Fratres*. This magazine and later publications by Rev. William Busch and Rev. Gerald Ellard were read and studied by every Sister as well as by many students in the Department of Religion at the College. Also in 1926 two Sisters [SISTER HYACINTH FLEMING AND ANOTHER SISTER, ED.] went to New York to attend the Pius X School of Sacred Music, where both Dom Moquereau and Mrs. Justine Ward were on the faculty. On their return, the Sisters introduced "Ward Singing" in some of the parochial schools. In September 1927 a course entitled "The Sacrifice and Ceremonies of the Mass" was entered on the College program. The course is not listed in the catalog of

College students had no regular choir, but they learned to sing Gregorian melodies in the choral classes. They also had weekly practices in the *Missa Recitata* and could now participate more effectively in both Low and High Masses, "alternating their voices with the priest and the choir according to the prescribed norms" (Pius XII Sect. 192).

In 1928 the Community had its first all-liturgical retreat. In 1929 and 1931 the Sisters attended the liturgical summer school at St. John's Abbey. During the fall of 1931 Prior Hammenstede of Maria Laach Abbey in Germany gave a four-day institute on "The Concept of the Liturgy." He was a vital teacher and impressed his hearers with a deeper appreciation of corporate worship and of the essential union of the Sacraments with the

Tower Hall in the 1930s

Mystical Body of Christ. Up to this time, on school days the students had been receiving Holy Communion before Mass. Thenceforth, the sacred Rite took its proper place, after the Communion of the celebrant.

Between 1935 and 1943 Rev. Norbert Gertken, OSB, of St. John's Abbey conducted three summer courses in Congregational Singing and *Schola*. Evidently, the College profited by these instructions, for the catalog of 1937 informed its patrons that at the Holy Sacrifice, "the *Missa Recitata* is the rule on ferial days. On Sundays and feast days the congregation sings the Mass in Gregorian Chant . . . on several occasions throughout the year, the students sing a part Mass." Thus while plainsong was given the preference, not only the Georgian but also polyphonic singing (the usual accompaniment of the sacred rites in the parish churches) was adequately taught.

The practice was in keeping with the circumstances and the needs since many of the College students were potential choir directors, organists, or singers in parish churches, and as graduates of The College of St. Scholastica, could rightly be expected to understand both polyphony and Gregorian music.

Between 1943 and 1952 the study of and participation in the liturgy was accelerated. Every summer experts were invited to give workshops or summer courses on organ, chant, or the Divine Office. Father Francois Lefevre conducted a workshop on congregational music and *schola* singing. Father Bernard Eamon and his associates held an institute for local organists and choir directors, both religious and lay. The College formed three *scholae*: one from members of the faculty, one composed of College girls, one of girls from Stanbrook Hall High School. Each *schola* took its turn in singing the High Mass. A group from the College organized a special choir, and when invited by pastors, went to sing the Sunday Mass in churches having no regular choir. Father Emeric Lawrence, OSB, came from St. John's Abbey to teach the Psalms; a priest from Conception Abbey came to instill a more correct rendering of the *Opus Dei.* High Masses increased in number to two or three a week. A class of science students began to chant *Compline* as their offering of prayer and praise at day's end. On Easter Sunday, 1951, the sung Vespers were introduced. At last, the liturgy was an established fact at St. Scholastica.

THE OFFICIAL PRAYER OF THE CHURCH

The *Opus Dei,* or Divine Office, prayed by Benedictines the world over, is now chanted in English by the Sisters. As a consequence, this beautiful prayer has become more familiar to all residents at St. Scholastica. They have learned that the Church, by the medium of certain chosen members, performs an unceasing office of prayer, wherein through the inspired poetry of the Psalms, she voices the praise and adoration of the Divine Majesty. It is not unusual to hear a student say: "If I had a religious vocation, I would love to say the Divine Office." There is no doubt that its rendering in the vernacular has made it more attractive. In slowly increasing numbers students come spontaneously to take part in *Compline* and the Sunday Vespers.

THE INFLUENCE OF THE LITURGY ON THE STUDENTS

"The primary and indispensable source of the true Christian spirit is the active participation in the most holy mysteries and in the public and solemn prayer of

Tower Hall in the 1940s

the Church." These remarkable words of Pius X in 1903 have been the rallying cry for a return to liturgy. Effort has been made by the College administration to create conditions that enable our students to live an intelligent liturgical life. A four-hour course in Sacred Liturgy is required of all Catholics. In this course, which is both historical and practical, formal teaching is vitalized by concrete demonstration of liturgical practices and the use of photochromatic slides. The Sisters are convinced that the study of the liturgy has effected a great change in the students' attitude toward the worship of God. The consciousness of being members of the Mystical Body has given them an added appreciation of the life of grace and has developed in them a sense of nearness to Christ. This helps them to forget their own little difficulties, to forgive injuries, and to supernaturalize their motives. A student nurse, when asked whether she had found the doctrine of the Mystical Body helpful in her profession, gave this reply: "O Sister, it has been a wonderful contribution in my practical work as a nurse. When patients come in, unkempt and hard to care for, I can always spiritualize the task, seeing Christ in them!"

The Chapel exercises are arranged at times when all who desire to participate can conveniently be present. To all this, the students have responded in a manner most gratifying. Daily attendance at Mass and the reception

The Chapel of Our Lady Queen of Peace in the 1940s

of Holy Communion, always quite high, is particularly good during Advent, the months of October and May, and during Lent. The same is true of attendance at the yearly novenas: The Immaculate Conception, St. Scholastica, St. Benedict, and the Church Unity octave. Great interest is manifested in the liturgical processions on Candlemas Day, Palm Sunday, and Corpus Christi, and in the functions of The Blessed Virgin Sodality—two of which are the traditional Crowning of our Blessed Mother on "College Mother's Day" and the "Rose Procession" on the Feast of Christ the King. In the latter function, each student places a rose in front of the altar before the Offertory of the Mass, thus symbolizing her love for Christ in the Blessed Sacrament.

Organ

In his *Encyclical on Sacred Music* of December 8, 1903, Pope Pius X writes: "Although the music proper to the Church is purely vocal music, music with accompaniment of the organ is also permitted" (qtd. in Predmore 7). And Pope Pius XI, reiterating the thought of his predecessor, writes as follows in his *Apostolic Constitutions on Sacred Music*:

> The traditionally appropriate musical instrument of the Church is the organ, which by reason of its extraordinary grandeur and majesty, has been considered a worthy adjunct to the liturgy. . . . Let our churches resound with

Stanbrook Hall, the Gymnasium in the rear, the Chapel of Our Lady Queen of Peace, and Tower Hall in the 1940s

organ music that gives expression to the majesty of the edifice and breathes the sacredness of the religious rites; in this way the art, both of those who build organs and of those who play them, will flourish afresh and render effective service to the sacred liturgy. (qtd. in Predmore 185)

At the College the organ has always been used except during penitential seasons and days when organ music is not permitted. At these times the choir sings *a capella*. For many years, the College had only a small reed organ as an adjunct to singing. Finally, in 1927 a generous donor who wished to remain anonymous gave the school a two-manual Kilgen organ suitable to the limited dimensions of the Chapel. This much-appreciated gift enhanced the Church's song at St. Scholastica, and the girls, now well instructed in the chant, joined their voices to those of the other singers in the pews.

When the new buildings were opened in 1938 and the former Chapel was converted to a music hall, the Kilgen remained in its accustomed place and became a practice instrument for students taking organ lessons. Again a reed organ did duty for singing until 1949, when an instrument worthy of the Chapel took its place.

The following article from the *Duluth Catholic Register* of June 19, 1949, refers to what was probably the outstanding event at St. Scholastica in 1949—the installation and dedication of a beautiful pipe organ and the first public organ concert in the Chapel. It reads:

The Cassavant organ recently installed in Our Lady Queen of Peace Chapel at The College of St. Scholastica will be dedicated on Sunday, June 26. After the blessing of the organ by the Most Reverend Thomas A. Welch and Benediction of the Blessed Sacrament, an organ recital

A music major directs choir for Mass in the late 1940s.

The crowning of Mary in the Chapel of Our Lady Queen of Peace was an annual May ceremony into the 1950s.

will be presented by Mario Salvador of St. Louis, Missouri, one of the most noted concert organists of today. A special *Tantum Ergo*, dedicated to the Benedictine Sisters, has been composed for the occasion by Mr. Salvador ("Scholastica's New Organ"). [When the original chapel was renovated in 1986, the organ was replaced. Ed.]

Liturgical Practices in the Parish Schools

Questionnaire

An encouraging aspect of the liturgical training at St. Scholastica is the influence it exerts outside the College. Most of the young Sisters become teachers in the parish or other schools staffed by the Community. Through them, every year a knowledge of the liturgy and its practices is channeled to the thousands of pupils whom they train and in some degree also to the students' families. This fact is evidenced in the answers to a questionnaire sent to the music teachers in twenty-six of the schools in September 1954. The questionnaire contained ten items relative to their teaching of the liturgy. These items were followed by a request for careful answers and a comment on the results achieved, the comment to be given by the music teacher or the principal. The items may be judged by the replies, which are summarized below.

Of the twenty-six teachers given the questionnaire, all but four reported on the questions either orally or in writing. Two others were teaching in catechetical centers to which the children came on released time from the public schools. The Sisters instructed them as they came, but the time of classes was short and the groups quite large. As one Sister explained in her report: "In these lightning periods we have no time for the liturgy. The most we can do is to teach the catechism."

REPLIES AND COMMENTS

In all the schools that answered the questionnaire, Gregorian chant is regularly sung, and all the pupils are instructed in the use of the Missal. The boys of the four upper grades in all the parish schools are taught to serve Mass and assist at other functions around the altar. All the pupils learn the Benediction hymns. Eighty-five percent sing a High Mass on weekdays and sing most of the Requiem Masses. Seventy-seven percent participate in the singing of the services of Christmas, Lent, and Holy Week. Sixty-one percent sing a High Mass every Sunday. In sixty percent of the schools, several of the girls are trained to play the organ for the various services. Forty-six percent pray the *Missa Recitata* on days when there is a Low Mass.

In the 1950s College of St. Scholastica students placed a rose in front of the altar in a special ceremony on the Feast of Christ the King.

The most frequent comment of the teachers is: "Our pupils love to sing"; of visitors or parents: "I like to attend the pupils' Mass; they sing with earnestness, and seem to understand perfectly what they sing." A teacher writes: "We have no Catholic high school in this town, so our pupils (after finishing the eighth grade), attend the public high school, but most of them wish to continue in the choir, and we make them welcome." The principal of a school that opened in September 1953 comments: "Last spring the choir director of a large church in Iowa was present at our school High Mass and remarked afterwards on the apparent facility with which we had gotten our pupils to sing the chant, whereas he can hardly 'drill' it into his adult choir. We had to smile, knowing that the 'facility' was indeed only 'apparent.'" From the singing teacher in one of our large city schools comes this interesting information: "We always have congregational singing at the children's Sunday Mass. Last year the parents, wishing to join in the singing, bought the Gregorian books and hired a liturgist to train them in the chant. This year they sing the nine o'clock Mass with the children. They say they want to make it a 'family Mass.'" The music teacher of a school that rated one hundred percent in all answers made the following comment: "I am new here this year, so I shall only give you my impression of the *Missa Recitata* here. It is very well developed. The children pray it beautifully and the adults also. The children, not the Sisters, lead the prayers. Adults pray the *Missa Recitata* at the earlier Masses on Sundays."

But in this as in every other good work, there are some drawbacks. A principal writes: "We haven't done much with our church singing the last few years. Our

Stanbrook Hall, the Chapel of Our Lady Queen of Peace, and Tower Hall in the 1950s

pastor prefers Low Masses on all weekdays, and the adult choir sings the Sunday High Mass (which is not in Gregorian Chant). We sing only the Requiem Masses and Benediction and sometimes English hymns." From St. Gertrude's School of Arts and Crafts comes the following: "Our children love to sing, but, as you know, we have no accommodation for an organ in our Chapel, and the children are slow to learn. It took an entire year, with constant practice, for them to learn one Mass and the Benediction hymns. These they now sing well. Mrs. Justine Ward was present recently at our Benediction and afterwards expressed her amazement at the excellent quality of their voices."

A large diocesan high school in which the liturgy seems to be diligently pursued and appreciated has a difficulty of another sort. The singing teacher writes: "We have a large mixed choir and two *scholae*: a girls', which I direct, and a boys', directed by the Reverend

Principal of the school. We sing the school Mass on certain Fridays and feast days. On these occasions, the singing is congregational. But since the students come from all the different parishes of the city, we haven't yet succeeded in getting them together for a Sunday High Mass. The idea appeals to the boys and girls, and we believe that if they could come at least one Sunday a month for this purpose, the experience would serve a two-fold end: an approach to the ideal of the *Missa Cantata* and the preparation of several nuclei of young and enthusiastic singers for the High Mass in the different parish churches."

All in all, much is being done. By courage, perseverance, and hard work much more can be accomplished. The road to perfection—even relative perfection—is an uphill road and is beset with many difficulties. To our zealous teachers of the liturgy we say: "Keep on climbing. *Ad astra per aspera.*"

X. Statuary of the College and Monastery

Within the buildings and on the campus of the College and Monastery, there are many fine pieces of statuary, some of them purchased by the administration, others acquired through the generosity of friends. The dual purpose of this chapter is to make all of these pieces more significant to our students by telling something of their history and characteristics and, if they are donations, to record in a permanent way the names of the donors. They are treated in the order of their acquisition.

STATUES IN WOOD (EARLY STYLES)

ST. SCHOLASTICA AND ST. BENEDICT

Standing within two richly carved shrines in the lobbies of the east cloister walk are the figures of our patrons, St. Benedict and St. Scholastica. An interesting history enhances their value. They were purchased by the founders of the Benedictine Community of Duluth in 1895 for the Chapel of the Sacred Heart Institute. There they remained until 1909, when it was thought proper to remove them to the "Villa," since the Sisters had chosen St. Scholastica as patroness of their new academy. At that time a heavy coating of gesso and black paint gave the figures the appearance of being plaster molds, but, in 1939 when suitable statues were contemplated for each end of the main cloister walk, the discovery was made that these historic pieces were genuine "objects of art." Mr. Maguolo, an Italian sculptor now curator of the

St. Louis Museum of Fine Arts, restored the pieces and appraised them as follows: "They were carved from white pine by a skilled craftsman, most likely a Saxon or Bavarian, about the year 1820. Seventy-five years later, when they had seen much wear, and wood sculpture had lost popularity even in Germany, they were treated with gesso and paint and exported to America as plaster statues. In 1895 plaster statuary was in great demand in this country."

Their story known, the antique pieces now became the object of general appreciation.

This wooden statue of St. Scholastica stood at the entrance to the College for many years.

The College sophomores and juniors, sponsoring the erection of St. Scholastica in the east cloister walk, obtained for her a beautiful shrine, hand-carved in Early Christian and Romanesque motifs and polychromed in red, green, brown, and gold. In the following spring, 1940, St. Scholastica was enshrined in the east cloister walk, at the entrance of Tower Hall.

For nearly ten years Scholastica's companion statue found a place in one of the reception rooms, but finally in 1948 the students of Stanbrook Hall High School gave St. Benedict a shrine exactly like that of St. Scholastica. It was erected at the other end of the main cloister walk, the entrance to Stanbrook Hall. Since then these two sainted founders of the Order have stood as guardians over the most traveled road within the College. Seeing them in this relation daily, we are impelled to study and compare them as works of art. They are neither saintly types nor realistic persons but a healthy balance between these two extremes. Their sanctity comes out in the utter sincerity of their attitudes, their downcast eyes, their evident humility. We know, however, that they were of Roman blood, the son and daughter of a patrician family (Schuster Ch. 5). This fact is brought to our attention in the dignity of the figures, in the strong, fine hands of Benedict, and in the simple grace with which Scholastica wears her habit. The brother and sister are portrayed in their mature years,

This wooden statue of St. Benedict stood at the entrance to Stanbrook Hall for many years.

though Benedict looks older than Scholastica. Her face is altogether serene; his is somewhat troubled. Perhaps the sculptor wanted to remind us of the prophecy in which, as St. Gregory relates, the holy founder learned of the destruction of his monastery, which was to occur half a century after his death (Gregory I 44). [For the current location of these statues, see Appendix A. Ed.]

Sacred Heart, Immaculate Conception, St. Joseph of the Lily

Three statues of smaller dimensions are valued for their connection with the early history of the school as well as for their use in illustrating a naturalistic trend in statuary all too common in every period of art. They are thirty inches high, carved from pine and painted in delicate tones of gray and buff, and elaborately bordered with gold. They were made in Munich and were brought from there to the Sacred Heart Institute in 1895. Although the figures give evidence of care on the part of their makers, they lack the sincerity of feeling that must characterize true art. They are pretty rather than beautiful. The over-delicate features of the faces, the artificial pose of the bodies and limbs, and the fussiness of the garments illustrate the taste that prevails in religious art when the spiritual has been displaced by the sentimental. Unhappily, all countries in the West have yielded to such decadence at certain periods. [The current location of these statues is unknown. Ed.]

St. Benedict and St. Scholastica (Gothic style)

During the Christmas season of 1925 the most Reverend Bishop Mc-Nicholas, then Bishop of Duluth, presented the Sisters with two beautiful statues of St. Benedict and St. Scholastica that he had obtained in Brussels, Belgium, during a visit to that city. The figures with their accompanying canopies and brackets were executed from fine cypress. They are in the Early Gothic art style, the accessories being polychromed in deep blue, vermillion, dark green, and gold, the preferred colors of Early Gothic art. Each set, arranged in its place on the wall, is forty inches in height, the figures alone measuring twenty inches.

Both saints are dressed in the Benedictine choir cloak, the vertical folds relieved by the gold borders and by the coordinating influence of faces and hands as well as by the white beard of Benedict and the white coif of Scholastica. The minute realism of the Gothic is seen in the soft texture of the garments and especially in the natural rendering: the eyes are real, the faces are modeled as flesh, the hands are strong and well made, and the feet are shapely but rather too small, a characteristic feature of figure sculpture during this period. On her right arm, across her waist, St. Scholastica holds a dove tinted in delicate blue; on her left, a book fastened with gold clasps. St. Benedict is looking straight ahead with earnest gaze, as if addressing a listening audience. He holds at his breast a book opened outward, and with the forefinger of his right hand points to these opening words inscribed in Latin on the pages of the book: *Ausculta, fili, mi praecepta magistri* ("Listen, my son, with attention to the precepts of your master") (St. Benedict, Prologue).

Gothic wooden statues of St. Scholastica and St. Benedict

Very interesting are the canopies and brackets in their gay coloring. (See page 108.) They are topped by pointed finials with crockets and patterned in tracery, as in Gothic windows. The relief is undercut in deep blue and edged in red and gold.

It might seem at first glance that there is some incongruity in placing sixth century saints in a thirteenth century setting, but it will become obvious, on second thought, that saints like these are timeless. St. Scholastica with her dove, recalling to a forgetful world the lesson of moral purity, may appear with equal urgency in the sixth century or the thirteenth or the twentieth. St. Benedict in every age has kept pleading for a return to Christ: "If you will have true and everlasting life, keep your tongue from evil and your lips that they speak no guile . . . seek after peace and pursue it. And when you have done these things, My eyes shall be upon you and My ears open to your prayers" (St. Benedict, Prologue). [For the current location of these statues, see Appendix A. Ed.]

STATUES IN MARBLE, STONE, & CERAMIC

OUR LADY OF GRACE (MARBLE STATUE)

This Cararra marble figure, fifty-four inches in height, carved in Italy, was imported in 1930 by the students of the Blessed Virgin Sodality and presented to their Alma Mater as the memorial gift of that year. It stands against the wall at a focal position in the first floor corridor of Tower Hall. At its right and left are the doors opening from the main lobby; directly in front is the central staircase leading to the different floors. Occupying this position, a converging point for students going to and coming from classes, Our Lady of Grace exerts a vital influence on the life of the College.

For the first two years after its erection, the figure rested on a sturdy oaken table. Then the Sodality and senior class of 1932 decided that Our Lady of Grace should have appointments in harmony with her beauty and importance. As a result of a second importation, their Patroness was given a pedestal of *verde* marble to stand upon and a Castilian marble vase to receive daily offerings of flowers. Shortly afterwards a dossal of royal blue velvet was draped from ceiling to floor behind the figure. The beautiful indoor shrine became the scene of two devotions that have since become traditional: every year on the Sodality Mothers' Day the resident students hold a crowning ceremony for Our Lady of Grace, and every evening during Mary's month they gather around the shrine to sing hymns in her honor. [FOR THE CURRENT LOCATION OF THIS STATUE, SEE APPENDIX A. ED.]

One of two canopies that once accompanied the Gothic statues of St. Scholastica and St. Benedict (see previous page)

The marble statue of Our Lady of Grace

The Archangel Gabriel (Stone Statue)

Ordinarily when angels appear in art, they fill a subordinate role; often their function is purely decorative. Not so the Archangels. As envoys of the royal majesty of God, they are clothed with a dignity befitting their mission. That is how the Archangel Gabriel appears in the Angelus Court, an enclosed garden between Tower Hall and the Chapel of Our Lady Queen of Peace. Gabriel stands in a recession of the east wall of the Chapel against a background of ornamental brickwork. High above him is the Angelus bell. Under his feet is an octagonal pedestal constructed from alternating layers of red brick and white limestone; over his head is a canopy, cone-shaped like the belfry, and like it, covered with antique copper. A wide stone molding at the base of the canopy is divided into eight squares lined with bright copper and ornamented with four-pointed stars.

The stone statue of Archangel Gabriel

The Archangel is carved from white Bedford stone. His wings, rising slightly above his shoulders, spread out behind him, then taper gracefully to the feet. They are modeled from narrow bands of stone that overlap each other and then taper to a point like the petals of a water lily. Under the wings he wears a cope. It is cast in broad lines and is fastened in front by a *morse*. He carries on his left arm not the usual trumpet but an Annunciation Lily, since his mission in this representation is to announce to the Virgin Mary that she is chosen to be the Mother of the God-Man. Of this sublime mystery we are reminded three times a day at the ringing of the Angelus. The figure of the Archangel is eight feet in height. With its pedestal and canopy, it gives the Angelus Court an impressive feature. It was designed by Mr. J. B. Hills of Delano, Minnesota, and carved by Mr. Victor Berlinger of St. Louis, Missouri.

The stone statue of Queen of the Lake greets visitors at the entrance to the Chapel of Our Lady Queen of Peace.

QUEEN OF THE LAKE (STONE STATUE)

This beautiful statue, sculptured from white Bedford limestone, also by Mr. Victor Berlinger of St. Louis, has been named "Queen of the Lake" because of its regal appearance and its commanding position overlooking the broad waters of Lake Superior. It reposes on a solid block of limestone before the main entrance of the Chapel, backed by the stone *trumeau* that divides the pair of double doors. Its height is ten feet; its diameter eighteen inches. Because of its slenderness, it might be thought at first glance to be a creation of the Beuronese School of Art, but one will note on closer inspection that the face has a more human appeal than is found in the Beuronese figures of the Blessed Virgin. It is said to resemble in a small way Our Lady of Chartres, although neither the Sisters nor the artist had that celebrated example in mind when the Queen of the Lake was designed.

The statue is an entirely original creation. It suggests a Benedictine influence in the graceful choir cloak that drapes the form as well as in the dove resting on Our Lady's right hand, raised toward the left shoulder, and in the olive branch held in her left hand. The dove and the olive branch are symbolic of "Peace," a traditional motto of Benedictinism. The preeminent sanctity of Our Lady and her universal queenship are signified: the first by a halo adorned with four-pointed stars, the second by a crown carved in the stone at some distance above the head.

ST. THOMAS MORE AND CARDINAL NEWMAN (CERAMIC STATUES)

On the east wall of the reference room of the College library are two triptych shrines made of golden oak. The one on the left contains a statue of St. Thomas More; that at the right, a statue of Cardinal Newman. The figures, thirty inches high, were designed in ceramic by Miss Margaret Stierlen of the Institute of Fine Arts, Chicago, Illinois. The purchase of these two interesting statues was sponsored by the Blessed Virgin Sodality of the College during the years 1942-1944 inclusive. [FOR THE CURRENT LOCATION OF THESE STATUES, SEE APPENDIX A. ED.]

ST. THOMAS MORE

The artist has represented St. Thomas More as he appears in his portrait as Lord Chancellor by Hans Holbein, made probably in 1527 when More was forty years of age. He is the typical gentleman scholar of the sixteenth century. The figure is robed in a deep purple gown that falls in semicircular folds over the instep, partly exposing the slippered feet. A collar of grey fur (probably sable) and short, fur-trimmed over-sleeves give elegance to the dress, while a metal chain around the neck and a signet ring on the index finger indicate the noble lineage of the wearer as well as his high position in the kingdom of England. It is interesting to note that the chain ends in a double rose pendant, an ornament the English Chancellor held in much affection as a mark of his devotion to his country's history.

St. Thomas More

CARDINAL NEWMAN

The Cardinal stands facing front, clothed in a scarlet-trimmed black cassock, *mozzetta*, and scarlet sash. His great dignity in the Church is indicated by the sapphire ring on his finger and the cardinal's hat molded in his coat of arms. A large pectoral cross hangs outside the *mozzetta* and reaches to his waist. Hands, sensitive and well formed, convey the impression of intellectual strength. The left hand falls at the side; the right, crossing at the waist, holds a book, suggestive of Newman's literary activities. Both face and figure, though delicate, indicate great firmness. The head is well poised, the nose aquiline, the eyes deep set, the chin broad, the mouth closed. Snow-white hair, partly concealed by the *zucchetto*, gives emphasis to the refined dignity of the face and figure.

At the base of the statue is Newman's coat of arms: a golden shield with three hearts and his literary motto, *Cor ad cor loquitur* ("Heart speaks to heart").

In the portrayal of More's personal traits, the statue accords well with this famous description of him in a letter written by Erasmus in 1519 to a fellow humanist, Ulrich von Hutten:

> To begin with what is best known to you, in stature he is not tall, though not remarkably short. His complexion is white, his face fair rather than pale; a faint flush of pink appears beneath the whiteness of the skin. His hair is dark brown or brownish-black; his eyes, greyish-blue. . . . His countenance is in harmony with his character, being always expressive of an amiable joyousness, and even an incipient laughter. (Burton 690)

Cardinal Newman

STATUES IN WOOD
(CONTEMPORARY STYLES)

Today when wood sculpturing is receiving the appreciation it deserves, the Germans of the Western zone are pursuing it again with increasing interest. In Bavaria especially there are many sculptors who produce really good creations in boxwood, cypress, pine, oak, and other native woods. From that country in 1951 and 1952 the Sisters imported the three pieces described next.

CHRIST THE KING

From Oberammergau in Upper Bavaria, a region renowned since the tenth century for its wood carving, this figure of Christ the King came to the College in the summer of 1951. The sculptor, Hans Heinzeller, executed it after a list of suggestions submitted by the Sisters, thus creating a truly original work.

The figure, fifty-two inches in height, now stands in a wall niche in the main floor of Tower Hall where its characteristic features as now given are shown to good advantage: a medium of fine boxwood, slightly off natural color; a figure of graceful and rather slender lines; vestments falling in expressive folds; majestic posture; a crowned head and benign countenance—all adding up to the impression of an

Contemporary wooden statue of
Christ the King

ideal king. In His left hand Christ holds the traditional orb, symbol of the redeemed world; with His right, raised aloft, He blesses that world of which He is Redeemer and King. [FOR THE CURRENT LOCATION OF THIS STATUE, SEE APPENDIX A. ED.]

HOLY FAMILY
(CHRISTMAS CRÈCHE)

By the same artist, Hans Heinzeller, and in the same medium, is a second subject, ordered by the Sisters after receiving the first statue. It is a life-like conception of Jesus, Mary, and Joseph as they appeared in the stable of Bethlehem on that first Holy Night before the coming of the Magi and the Shepherds; it serves as a Nativity group in the Monastic Chapel from Christmas Eve to the close of the Christmas season.

Naturally, the most interesting of the figures of the trio is that of the Infant Jesus, "Wrapped in swaddling clothes" (Luke 2:7). In this instance, He lies on an elliptical pallet carved from boxwood, yet the artist has contrived to give to the blanket under His sacred Body the cast of soft wool, and to the rough border of the pallet an appearance of real straw. All the figures are executed with loving carefulness—the face, hands, and feet of the Infant being especially good. Mary kneels at the head of the crib, her hands folded in prayer, her eyes fixed ecstatically on the Child. St. Joseph, a staff in his right hand, a lantern in his left, stands guard over Mother and Child. The group constitutes a beautiful ideal of the unity and mutual love that should characterize a Christian family. [FOR THE CURRENT LOCATION OF THESE STATUES, SEE APPENDIX A. ED.]

THE CRUCIFIX

A third piece from the Heinzeller studio is a crucifix, the cross of which is forty-eight inches high and made from oak; the *Corpus* is twenty-two inches high and made from white pine. The piece was selected for the north dining room by two Sisters who visited Oberammergau during the Holy Year of 1950. [SISTER ALICE LAMB AND SISTER BENEDICT BIRKHOLZ, ED.]

In this crucifixion scene the sacred Body is thrust forward, tensing the arm muscles to such an extent that they appear to be almost dislocated; the hair under the crown of thorns is matted with blood. The sacred Face is marked with suffering. Yet neither the Face nor the Body of our Redeemer is in any way distorted. Studying them, one realizes in some measure what must have been the agony of those tragic three hours. Yet underneath

the marks of anguish a supernatural beauty shines out, recalling the words of our Savior in His last instruction to the people: "And I, if I be lifted up, will draw all to Myself" (John 12: 32). [FOR THE CURRENT LOCATION OF THE CRUCIFIX, SEE APPENDIX A. ED.]

CAMPUS SHRINES AT ST. SCHOLASTICA

To make the grounds more interesting and to implement its teaching on our Savior and his Blessed Mother, the College has erected several outdoor shrines upon the West Campus. They are located along shaded pathways at some distance from each other. In May and in the milder weathers generally, individuals and groups among the Sisters and the College girls may be seen making a daily pilgrimage to one or other of these sacred places. Following are short descriptions of the most popular shrines.

PIETA

In the Monastery cemetery is a stone sculpture based on Michelangelo's Pieta in St. Peter's Cathedral in Rome. Next to the Madonna and Child, the Pieta has been the most popular subject in all religious art, more than sixty of the great masters

Crucifix (top) and the Holy Family statues from the Heinzeller studio. The Holy Family statues are shown in front of a copper Screen created by Sister Constantina Kakonyi.

The Pieta in the Monastery cemetery

having interpreted it in painting or sculpture. Our Pieta is a copy of one of Michelangelo's creations.

Our Lord's body is completely relaxed, showing that it has been taken down from the Cross. It is supported by the Blessed Mother kneeling on one knee at His left. Her right arm is under the Sacred Head, which is turned to the right and thrown slightly backward. His right arm falls limp at the side. Both pierced feet were evidently nailed as one, for the instruments of torture lying on the base include only three nails.

In this, as in Michaelangelo's other interpretations of the subject, the Blessed Mother is considerably larger than the Crucified Lord—a device used to place emphasis on her great affliction. The sense of loss, of compassion, of resignation is expressed in her whole person as she gazes upon her beloved Son, dead in her arms. Yet there is no weakness in her face or form. Better than any other human being, she realizes the meaning of and the need for our Redemption.

The Sacred Heart Shrine
Closer to the College is a much-frequented shrine of our Savior. It has its locus on the face of the cliff from which the granite was quarried for the Villa and gymnasium.

The stone is gouged out concavely from the cliff, except at the center, where it was hewn into a high pedestal for a statue. Low trees and shrubs above the cliff, a lovely rock garden at its base, and a natural flight of steps cut into the rock at either side create a natural framework for the shrine development. The formation is thirty feet wide and forty feet high, a spacious and delightful setting for the twelve-foot figure of the Sacred Heart.

In June 1909 this massive statue, carved from white limestone, was presented to the Sisters of St. Benedict's Hospital, Grand Rapids, Minnesota, by Reverend Louis Buecheler. When the hospital closed in 1912, the Sisters shipped it to the Villa and, on the completion of the site in 1946, it was conveyed to its present place. On its high pedestal the tall, white figure with its bent head and outstretched arms conveys most vividly

The Sacred Heart Shrine (top) and a photo of novices preparing the gardens surrounding the Sacred Heart Shrine

the invitation of the Sacred Heart of Jesus, whom the statue represents: "Come to Me, all you who labor and are heavily burdened and I will refresh you" (Matthew 11:28).

One of the highlights of the laywomen's retreats, usually held every year in August, is a candlelight procession to this Shrine.

OUR LADY OF VICTORY

One of our popular outdoor devotions is a visit to the shrine of Our Lady of Victory, located in Maryglade Park, a short walk from the College. The canopy and pedestal of this shrine are constructed of small varicolored stones gathered from along the beach of Lake Superior. Both the shrine and the stone cross surmounting it are entwined with vines and backed by clusters of spruce and elder, giving it a perfect natural setting. In front, flowers grow around

Students often visited the shrine of Our Lady of Victory for prayer and contemplation.

The enshrined statue represents the Blessed Mother with the Child Jesus at her right. The figures are two-thirds life-size, the Divine Child appearing to be about one year old. Our Lady stands majestically under a canopy, a crowned Queen with her little crowned King. Mother and Son seem to look benignly upon us as we kneel to pray for victory in our own undertakings and for victory over the forces of evil in the world.

The statue is modeled after an original work in the Parisian church of Our Lady of Victory founded by Louis XIII in 1628. Church and statue were Louis' thanksgiving offering for the royal victory over the Hugenots at La Rochelle. Although our statue is executed in terra-cotta, while the original work is in marble, it is an excellent reproduction, showing Late Renaissance influence and that unmistakable sense of style that has characterized French Art since the Middle Ages.

the pedestal, and some hand, lovingly devout, has set into the ground a row of flagstones to serve as kneeling benches for Our Lady's clients.

This fine piece was donated by Right Reverend Patrick Byrnes. [THIS STATUE AND SHRINE NO LONGER EXIST. ED.]

XI. Pictures in the College and Monastery

Over the years The College of St. Scholastica and the Monastery formed a fairly large collection of pictures by approved artists. They may be classified in a general way as oil paintings, water color paintings, and engraved prints. Representative pictures from each of these divisions are treated briefly in the following pages with a view to assisting the student in identifying the various types and in knowing what to look for in evaluating a picture.

OIL PAINTINGS

"OUR LADY OF REFUGE" (93" x 55") was painted by Gottfried Schiller of St. Louis, Missouri, formerly of Beuron Abbey, Germany. The theme is symbolic. It portrays Our Lady as a heroic figure, dominating the picture. Before her stands her Divine Son, whom she gently supports as He stretches His arms in the form of a cross, raising His right hand to bless us. He wears the dalmatic vestment, a sign of His priesthood, and stands upon a globe to indicate His sovereignty over the world, which is His footstool. Thus is symbolized the four-fold character of Mary's Son: Redeemer, Prince of Peace, High Priest, and King of the World.

The mantle of our Blessed Mother is held by angels at the upper right and left. They spread it out on either side, sheltering under the ample folds a group of figures that represents humanity seeking comfort and protection from the Mother of Jesus. [THIS PAINTING COULD NOT BE SALVAGED WHEN THE CHAPEL WAS RENOVATED. ED.]

"Our Lady of Refuge"

"SAINT JOSEPH" (93" x 55"), the companion painting of "Our Lady of Refuge," was made by the same artist, Gottfried Schiller. It represents St. Joseph, the central figure, as a man of regal build yet benign and humble in countenance and bearing. His left hand rests upon a carpenter's square, the instrument of his trade; his right hand points at once to heaven and to a scroll held by angels above his head. The legend of their scroll is the Benedictine motto, *Ora et Labora* (DeLatte 11), prayer and work, so perfectly exemplified in the life of St. Joseph. Directly in front of the saint stands the Divine Child, appearing as a boy of twelve. One notices a marked resemblance in face and figure between the Christ Child, His Mother in the other picture, and His foster father, St. Joseph. All were of the royal House of David, a fact symbolized in the Book of Kings, which the boy Christ holds at His breast, the open pages turned toward the beholder. Below, completing the theme of St. Joseph's role in the Holy Family and the Church, there are at right and left clusters of stylized lilies, signifying the saint's virginity. [THIS PAINTING COULD NOT BE SALVAGED WHEN THE CHAPEL WAS RENOVATED. ED.]

"THE LAST MEETING OF SAINT BENEDICT AND SAINT SCHOLASTICA" (65" x 33") portrays a touching scene, described in the following words by St. Gregory the Great in his *Second Book of Dialogues*:

> Accompanied by a few of his brethren, St. Benedict made his yearly visit to his twin sister Scholastica and spent the hours talking of God and of eternity. When the time for his departure drew near, Scholastica, because of a strange intuition that they would meet no more on earth, begged him to pass the night with her in further heavenly conversation. But when Benedict replied that it would be impossible for him to pass the night outside of his monastery, Scholastica bowed her head and prayed silently that he might stay. God's answer came in the form of a terrible storm that prevented the return of the monks. Scholastica raised her head and looked at her brother. "May Almighty God have pity on thee, my sister," said Benedict. "What has thou done?" "My brother," was the answer, "I entreated thee and thou wouldst not hear; I had recourse to my Lord, and He has had compassion on me and has heard my prayer. Go forth now if thou canst; leave me alone and return to thy monastery." (Forbes 104-105)

"The Last Meeting . . ." was painted after an unsigned etching in black and white. Its artist, Louis Gatey, of St. Louis, Missouri, followed the main lines of the

"Saint Joseph"

"The Last Meeting of Saint Benedict and Saint Scholastica"

"THE ASSUMPTION" (60" x 42"), a canvas by Susan Schoenfel, is an exact copy of one of Murillos' paintings of Our Lady. After its completion, this picture hung in a gallery of the Louvre beside its original until it was purchased for Mr. Eugene A. Shores of Ashland, Wisconsin, by his friend, Dr. Edgar Fairfield, our Ambassador to Paris, some fifty years ago. When the Shores' mansion was sold in 1938, Mrs. Shores Walker of Duluth, to whom "The Assumption" had come by inheritance, gave it to the Sisters.

Our Lady, exempt from the laws of gravitation, rises in natural motion, while the clouds beneath her spread outward and upward in a splendor of golden bronze and blue. She is no vaporous or illusory figure, but a personality replete with womanhood, while at the same time vitally and tenderly spiritual. [FOR THE CURRENT LOCATION OF THIS PAINTING, SEE APPENDIX A. ED.]

"ORA ET LABORA," a colossal mural painting representing the work of the Benedictine Sisters of Duluth, adorns the west wall of the reading room in the students' library (see p. 71). This particular wall area, in full view of all who enter the library from the east cloister walk, provides ample space for the twenty-five life-size figures that symbolize the varied activities of the Religious in prayer, Catholic action, teaching, nursing, scientific research, literary production, and fine arts.

The central figure is that of St. Benedict, founder of the Order; at his left, a large cross held by an altar boy divides the panel at its center and indicates the character of the painting. Mother Scholastica, foundress of the Benedictine Sisters in Duluth, stands at the other side of the cross, and St. Benedict, turned toward her, indicates by a gesture his approval of the many forms of apostolic work the Benedictines under her guidance have undertaken in the cause of Christian charity. The cross, the presence of the great Patriarch, the angels and the Benedictine mottos *Ora et Labora* ("Prayer and Work"), *In Omnibus Glorificetur Deus* ("In all things may God be glorified"), and *Pax* ("Peace") emphasize the mystical character of the theme.

etching but interpreted it freely. In a wonderful way he has caught the expression of rapture in the face of St. Scholastica when she realizes that her prayer is answered. [FOR CURRENT LOCATION OF THIS PICTURE, SEE APPENDIX A. ED.]

Very skillfully, the painter has included two of the library columns into her design in order to break the wide panels on either side of the cross and create the illusion of depth. Other techniques that give depth to the mural are the angels hovering in the distant background and a painting within a painting—that of Monte Cassino Abbey—at the upper right of St. Benedict. From the middle point, at the cross, the design spreads to left and right. The main pattern, formed by the nuns in their dark habits and white coifs, is relieved at proper intervals by altar boys, nurses, students, and children, dressed in white, rose, or blue—the whole achieving a balanced and harmonious composition.

A tall library window painted at each end of the mural gives it an effective frame. Through the window at the left is seen the Chapel; through the one at the right, Tower Hall. Sisters, postulants, students, and other persons passing up and down the entrance steps suggest that prayer and work are in progress at the College.

"The Assumption"

The painting is thirty-six feet wide and eight feet high. It was painted by Madame Maria Bartha, Instructor in Art at The College of St. Scholastica.

["ORA ET LABORA" NO LONGER EXISTS. AT THE TIME OF THE CHAPEL/LIBRARY RENOVATION IN 1986, IT HAD BECOME DAMAGED FROM THE EFFECTS OF HEAT, DRYNESS, AND DAMPNESS SURROUNDING IT AND COULD NOT BE SUITABLY REPAIRED. IT WAS, THEREFORE, TAKEN APART AND DESTROYED. ED.]

"THE VISIT OF THE MAGI" (51" x 41"), by Berni Quick of the Minneapolis School of Art, is a new interpretation of this sacred event. In the picture the Blessed Mother stands in an open loft of the stable beside a heap of straw on which lies the Infant Savior. At her right is St. Joseph, who hands her a rose—symbolic of love. The Magi, on the lower level of the stable, look up in adoration while presenting their gifts to the newborn King. Two Roman soldiers, who escorted the Wise Men from Jerusalem to Bethlehem at the command of Herod, and a dim cross in the distant background anticipate the crucifixion.

A star stands above the manger, angels on either side, and the precious gifts of the three kings conform to the traditional treatment of the subject. An original feature is seen in the blind shepherd boy who piteously looks up at the Mother and Child. He foreshadows the healing of the sick by Christ. [THE CURRENT LOCATION OF THIS PAINTING IS UNKNOWN. IT WAS RETURNED TO THE ARTIST BY SISTER AGNES SOMERS. ED.]

The following four beautiful paintings by Sister Constantina Kakonyi, artist at the College, present an original interpretation of the crucifixion of Our Lord, the mission of St. Benedict in the Christian world, the death of St. Scholastica, and the Madonna and Child.

"CONSUMMATUM EST" (60" x 40"), the crucifixion scene, is painted on a background of vermillion, thereby symbolizing the perils that threaten Christ's Mystical Body, the Church. The large Roman cross on which hangs the Crucified Redeemer and a panel thirty-three inches by thirty inches, extending below the horizontal beam of the cross, constitute the painting. In the left section of the panel stands the Blessed Mother; in the opposite section, the Beloved Disciple, St. John. Our Lord's head has fallen slightly to the side of His Mother, who looks directly out upon the world confided to her maternal care; St. John looks toward the Blessed Mother. Courage, suffering, love of mankind are symbolized by the attitudes and facial expression of the Mother and the Disciple chosen to be her protector. [FOR THE CURRENT LOCATION OF THIS PAINTING, SEE APPENDIX A. ED.]

"LIGHT IN THE DARKNESS" (56" x 40") shows St. Benedict as a youthful hermit, meditating in a solitary valley on a text of the Gospel Book he holds between his fingers. A wide beam of light encircling the upper part

"Consummatum Est"

"Light in the Darkness"

of singing angels at the upper right and lower left of the picture are arrayed in green and gold. The Saint's garments, brown where the shadows touch them, are vermillion in the better light. From an opening at the top, the canvas is bathed in a radiant light that surrounds the face and shoulders of the dying Saint and brings into relief the dove, poised on her clasped fingers. The ecstatic face, upturned to heaven, and the dove, symbol of the Holy Spirit, suggest the rapture of a pure soul anticipating from afar the glory of the Beatific Vision (Van Treeck and Croft 44).

In spite of the difference in their ages at the time they are represented in these pictures, the brother and sister bear a striking resemblance to each other, especially in their beautiful dark eyes and the spiritual ardor with which each one welcomes the vision vouchsafed to him or her. [FOR THE CURRENT LOCATION OF THIS PAINTING, SEE APPENDIX A. ED.]

of the valley lights up and glorifies the figure of the Saint. His head is turned to the left, his face uplifted to heaven from which has come the revelation of his mission. The nature of the message becomes evident to us as we study the upper background of the picture high above the Saint. There, on a rocky height, is the dim outline of a great monastery. From it will spring a thousand other spiritual powerhouses for the zeal of pontiffs, missionaries, holy men and women who will diffuse light in the darkness of paganism—old and new. [FOR THE CURRENT LOCATION OF THIS PAINTING, SEE APPENDIX A. ED.]

"LIGHT IN THE LIGHT" (56" x 40") shows Benedict's sister, St. Scholastica. She symbolizes dedication of the heart, as he symbolizes dedication of the mind. This picture portrays the death of St. Scholastica, not in terms of sadness and mourning, but in color and joy. Groups

"Light in the Light"

"The Madonna of Trust" (33" x 27") illustrates in an interesting way the paintings of Our Blessed Mother and the Divine Child executed in the late medieval period. It is not the Madonna and Child that we see in so many modern paintings—a doting mother of sentimental charm absorbed in a babe resembling herself. Here is a mother of simple yet strong personality, exalted in the sense of her greatness as Mother of the Messiah, yet humbly conscious of her mission as the lowly handmaid of God. In the Middle Ages, faith and humility went hand in hand.

Further emphasis is given to the medieval feeling by the strong black lines enclosing the figures, which are painted mostly in vivid reds and yellows, with their accompanying tints. The black outlines were a device used by Romanesque painters to enhance the color contrasts, to give the picture clearness of form and to bring the various elements into a harmonious unity. In this instance the device has been used most effectively by Sister Constantina Kakonyi, the painter of "Madonna of Trust."

As one studies the picture, the fitness of the title grows upon one. The Blessed Mother inclines toward her Son and Lord in an attitude of serene confidence as she supports His Body on her sturdy right arm. Meanwhile the Heavenly Babe, asleep on her breast in a posture relaxed and peaceful, reciprocates the attitude of

The Madonna and Child pictured here is one of several similar paintings by Sister Constantina Kakonyi.

His Mother. The spirit that results is one of mutual trust.

[THE LOCATION OF THE PICTURE DESCRIBED ABOVE IS UNKNOWN. FOR THE CURRENT LOCATION OF THE PAINTING PICTURED, SEE APPENDIX A. ED.]

"SAINT AGNES" (28"x 22") is a very old painting. Though the name of the painter is not inscribed, it has been identified by art critics as belonging to the school of Carlo Dolci, a school that painted only heads. "Saint Agnes" is portrayed in the manner of these painters. Her countenance wears a gentle and tender expression; yet hers is no weak or timorous piety. There is calm determination in the closed lips and the well-poised head. The picture (p. 124) is remarkable for the transparency of its coloring. [FOR THE CURRENT LOCATION OF THIS PAINTING, SEE APPENDIX A. ED.]

"THE EGYPTIAN FAIR" (28"x 42", painted by G. Marback in sultry tones of red, blue, orange, and green, conveys the colorful atmosphere that pervades an Arabian barter scene. Truculent dealers, cross-legged on the semiarid ground, haggle over values and prices. Scattered about are rugs, shawls, fruits, bric-a-brac. A turbaned figure with his back toward us dominates the foreground of the picture, while a placid camel at the back enjoys his moment of repose. This picture is an example of loaded painting. [THE CURRENT LOCATION OF THIS PICTURE IS UNKNOWN. ED.]

"Saint Agnes"

INDIVIDUAL PORTRAITS

Portraits of individuals arouse our especial notice when we are acquainted with the persons portrayed. A considerable number of portraits in oils are among our most interesting paintings. But since most of the subjects are connected with the history of the nation, the Church, or the Diocese of Duluth and its institutions, they are well known to the students and friends of the College. In every case, too, the name of the painter is inscribed on his painting. A written description of these personal portraits is therefore unnecessary.

Individual portraits were hung, as here in the Foyer Parlor, as well as in classrooms and hallways of Tower Hall.

LANDSCAPE PAINTINGS

Some years ago our government sent out a group of artists who were to find natural places unspoiled by human hands that might be set aside as parks having the character and distinctive spirit of American scenery. Whether any such places were discovered in Minnesota is not known to the writer. It would seem that our native State with its ten thousand lakes, its tree-bound streams, its rocky hillsides would provide examples full of character and spirit.

Many landscape pictures hang on the walls of The College of St. Scholastica and St. Scholastica Monastery. From among them, we have selected for special study seven paintings, five of which were painted by Minnesota artists.

Two canvases of Mr. Ralph Brewer of St. Paul, Minnesota, are illustrative of the character and spirit of contemporary landscape work.

"NOVEMBER AFTERNOON AT CHESTER CREEK" (36" x 30") shows a local beauty spot, glorified into a blaze of color by the full reflection of a red western sky. The jagged edges of the creek are softened by a new-fallen snow. Tall elms and birches, bare of leaves, have taken on hues of golden-brown and pink; snow, mauve-tinted, lies lightly on the shrubs and stones. The water is a bluish-green. A clear, still atmosphere pervades the scene. The character of this picture is serenity; its spirit is reverence. [FOR THE CURRENT LOCATION OF THIS PAINTING, SEE APPENDIX A. ED.]

"Winter in Tennessee" (31" x 25") is the title of the second landscape by this same artist. It pictures a lone cabin, set far back from the road and made more isolated by a grim mountain background. Behind the cabin, at the lower border of the mountain, is a thin line of scrub pine. A single pine in the foreground, irregular and dark-hued, intensifies the spirit of loneliness the scene is meant to express. [For the current location of this painting, see Appendix A. Ed.]

"Summer by the Lake" (40" x 40"), by Mr. Knute Heldner of the Minneapolis School of Art, presents nature under a totally different aspect. The time is about noon on a day that seems to be in the month of June or early July, since the trees are still in fresh leafage. Golden sunshine fills every open space, turning the green grass to an olive hue. One senses that no sound breaks the quiet, except perhaps that of a gentle breeze or the occasional hum of a bee. Even the stream that flows through clustered maples to join a crystal lake in the background makes only a sleepy murmur, for the curves of its waves are quite unruffled, and the lake is perfectly still. This picture conveys both the character and the spirit of "rest." [The current location of this painting is unknown. Ed.]

Two landscapes by Sister Salome Blais, Instructor of Art at the College, were painted from local subjects.

"Sand Dunes" (32" x 26") depicts very well the character of the sand formations on Lake Superior at Park Point. The spot is barren of vegetation except for some patches of sand cherry and a struggling tree or two. Above the burning heaps, a transparent blue sky and the cooling deep blue of the lake give a sense of refreshment. Life is imparted by the red berries on the bush and a white seagull darting back and forth above the water. Very interesting is the sand, reflecting its golden sheen under the bright sun of a noonday in August. [The current location of this painting is unknown. Ed.]

"Peonies" (24" x 18"), the second painting by Sister Salome, may be classified as a landscape. It is a flower picture. In this northern clime, flowers take on very vivid hues during the summer, and the artist has reproduced this quality in a subtle way without detracting from the delicate texture of the petals. Both these pictures are watercolors. [The current location of this painting is unknown. Ed.]

"Ballet of Ballianalula" (50" x 28") is an enchanting landscape, done in watercolor by John Falkner, a painter of Irish scenes. He has caught the fleeting lights and shadows that appear in swiftly moving water. The river moves on

"November Afternoon at Chester Creek" by Ralph Brewer

"Winter in Tennessee" by Ralph Brewer

with a rapid musical cadence, which suggests the liquid quality of its name, "Ballianalula." It broadens as it approaches us in the foreground of the picture, and the foamy bubbles are so real that one could almost imagine it possible to dip one's fingers into them. [THE CURRENT LOCATION OF THIS PAINTING IS UNKNOWN. ED.]

The first in a series of five historic Japanese woodcut prints titled "First Snowfall on Yedo"— the Monastery owns five prints from the series' eight woodcuts.

ENGRAVED PRINTS

Herbert Slater defines engraving as "The art of cutting metals, wood, and precious stones and representing on the face of any of them a design to be reproduced on suitable materials" (2). In popular usage, however, the term "engraving" is applied to an impression made from any of these mediums, and it is in the latter sense that the word is employed here.

Artists excepted, very few people know anything about printmaking. Yet good messotints, etchings, woodcuts, line engravings, and lithographs are classed with the highest forms of art. The mechanical color prints that flood the market at the present time should not obscure the fact that the graphic processes are capable of true artistic creation, whether the engravings so made be originals or after the paintings of other artists. Durer, Holbein, Rembrandt, Hogarth, Blake, Whistler all employed their genius in woodcuts, line engravings, etchings, and lithographs, often using the works of earlier artists as their inspiration.

To know how to distinguish the various types, as well as to determine a good from a poor or faked print, would seem to be a "must" for the educated person to-

day. Therefore the following explanation, given in connection with examples of the different types, is presented in order to induce the student to become interested in the art of engraving.

WOOD ENGRAVING OR WOODCUTS

A wood engraving, or woodcut as it is commonly called, is an impression made from a drawing cut in cameo on a block of wood. There are two methods of making woodcuts, namely, the black-line and white-line methods. In the first, the raised part of the wood is cut in facsimile; the cut-out part is disregarded. In the second, the process is reversed. Not all woodcuts are in black and white, however. Since 1625, when color engraving was invented, block printing in color has almost entirely displaced the black-and-white prints.

Of all the countries, Holland and Japan have been the most noted for their woodcuts. For the Japanese it is the national mode of art, and they have developed it to a peak of perfection. Even the masters there have used it as a direct form of art expression. In the Netherlands, too, the woodcut has been constantly popular, although the leading Dutch artists probably gave more attention to wood engravings in black and white than to the color prints. It is our good fortune to have representative woodcuts of both countries.

"OLD BRIDGE" (16" x 12") will be recognized at once as a white-line woodcut. It was made by W. O. J. Nieuvencamp, a Dutch engraver, who followed the art traditions of his countrymen. He was born at Amsterdam in 1867.

Four of the Monastery's five historic Japanese woodcut prints.

In its execution, the design of "Old Bridge" is both intricate and delicate. The curving rhythm of the river as it flows under the arches of the bridge and the perspective of the buildings on the other side are masterly and accurately portrayed. The lines suggest first the gradual, then the increased, rapidity of the stream as it descends a minor waterfall indicated by a horizontal shadow across the picture. [THE CURRENT LOCATION OF THIS ENGRAVING IS UNKNOWN. ED.]

"FIRST SNOWFALL IN YEDO" (16" x 12") is a series of eight woodcuts, giving as many views of that charming and colorful Japanese city as it appears the morning after an early and rather heavy snow. [The Monastery posseses five of the eight woodcuts. Ed.] The drawings were done in black and white by the famous artist Ichiryusai Hiroshige shortly before his death in 1858, but were not printed until nearly seventy years later. In the certified authentic document that accompanied the engravings, the following explanation is given for this delay:

> For some unknown reason the original sketches were mislaid at the time of Hiroshige's death and were not discovered until 1927, when immediate steps were taken to have engravings made from them. The work was then done by Yujiro Madea, Japan's most celebrated block-print engraver, in the very colors and tints he believed Hiroshige would have used. (Toto Yukemi Hakel)

The set was published in 1928, and shortly after that time the Sisters became the possessors of a first edition through the kindness of His Excellency, the Most Reverend Thomas A. Welch, who had just received it from the publisher, Shotaro Sato. In addition to having the interest of all true art creations, these prints are valuable for the wonderful manner in which they portray the Japanese spirit. One notes first of all the Japanese love of color and contrast in the disposition of reds and blues and yellows against the soft background of white snow; then their many-storied pagodas, their quaint houseboats, their artistic bridges, their low docks, their love of nature—especially of deep blue waters, cerulean skies, trees still heavy with leafage that falls in drooping clusters. But most interesting of all in these pictures are the persons—almost always men: an officious mandarin with buttoned hat; coolies carrying rickshaws; traders with yokes; and peasants, small of stature, weighed down with bundles, all of them trudging patiently through the snow that is everywhere.

First edition woodcuts are today collectors' items, and these are of high value, not only because they are first edition prints, but still more because they are a first edition of drawings made by Japan's master artist of wood engraving. [FOR THE CURRENT LOCATION OF THESE WOODCUTS, SEE APPENDIX A. ED.]

Sixteen of the original twenty etchings by Brother Notker of Maria Laach Abbey now hang on the third floor of Stanbrook. This one is titled "Roma, S. Maria in Trastevere."

LINE

ENGRAVING

A print made from a copper or steel plate on which a design has been incised in fine lines by special instruments and the furrows of these lines treated in ink is called a line engraving. Copper was the medium first used for this type, but it was replaced by steel about the year 1850 when it was discovered that a plate of much finer lines could be made with steel because of its greater density.

"THE LAST SUPPER" (42" x 25") is a steel engraving executed by A. L. Dick, who used Leonardo da Vinci's great painting as his inspiration. The engraving, though old, is in excellent condition. Fine, clear lines are employed throughout, except on the ridges of the faces where dots and dashes are used to heighten the general effect. Dick was an American artist, much appreciated in his time. He died in 1865. [THE CURRENT LOCATION OF THIS ENGRAVING IS UNKNOWN. ED.]

ETCHING

An etching is an impression taken from a metal plate—generally of copper—that has been prepared in this manner: the metal is first covered with an acid resistant such as varnish to form a ground; next, the lines of the design are drawn through the surface resistant onto the plate with a sharp instrument like a needle; then over the plate is poured an acid that bites into the parts where the surface has been exposed by the needle, leaving other parts untouched. Finally, a special kind of paper is impressed, and when it is drawn off it carries the etching.

Two etchings (40" x 27") that picture dramatic episodes in the city life of fifty or sixty years ago bear the titles "A WELCOME VISITOR" (the lover making his daily visit) and "HANGING OF THE CRANE." The first is by William Sartain after a painting by Anne Bronscombe; the second, by Hamel Hamilton after a painting by Francis Jones. Done in black and white, their clear, fresh look and masterly distribution of values make these prints fine examples of what a good etching should be. Although the details are realistic—faces, figures, and elegance of background all recalling the romantic style of the late nineteenth century—they show a fitting sincerity and restraint. Sartain and Hamilton were artists of English-American origin who did their best work about 1870. [THE CURRENT LOCATION OF THESE ETCHINGS IS UNKNOWN. ED.]

MEZZOTINT

"LADY TEMPLETON AND SON" (25"x 14"), by Richard Smythe, after Lawrence, is a good illustration of the mezzotint, a difficult and delicate type of engraving. In preparing the plate, rough lines are first burned on a copper or steel medium, which is then called a burred plate. This is covered with lampblack, and the design is transferred to it. Finally, the excess metal is scraped away, and the plate is burnished to produce the right degrees in lights and shades.

Richard Smythe worked entirely on mezzotints, a process in which he obtained excellent results. Most of his pictures are portraits of women, chiefly after Gainsborough, Reynolds, and Lawrence. He was an English artist, born in 1889. [THE CURRENT LOCATION OF THIS PICTURE IS UNKNOWN. ED.]

"ROMAN SCENES" (14" x 18") Along the ascending walls on either side of the double stairway in Tower Hall, there hangs a set of etchings executed in black and white. The series, numbering twenty in all, is by Brother Notker of the Maria Laach Abbey. They are taken from varied, though related, subjects: ancient ruins the Roman Forum, the Colliseum, the Arch of Constantine; Christian churches— St. Lawrence, St. Maria Major, SS. John and Paul, St. Cassitia, SS. Cosmas and Damien; famous palaces—the Vatican, the Palatine; celebrated walks and gardens—Via Appia, Piazza del Popolo, Galatean Gardens; and most interesting of all, perhaps, two famous Benedictine Abbeys—Monte Cassino as it appeared

"Roma, S. Pietro" (top) and "Roma, Interro del Quattra Coronati" (bottom), two of the etchings by Brother Notker that hang on the third floor of Stanbrook

before the war (World War II) and Maria Laach near Trier, Germany, as it is today.

While most of the subjects are of standing popularity, they are interpreted here from a new perspective. Also they show a more modern feeling in character and spirit, qualities so much appreciated in present-day art. [FOR THE CURRENT LOCATION OF THESE ETCHINGS, SEE APPENDIX A. ED.]

COLOR ETCHING

A method of making color etchings—putting the color onto the plate instead of coloring the impression by hand—was discovered in the late nineteenth century. Engravings done in this method enjoyed an immense popularity for a time and are still in rather wide demand. Two that represent the type are:

"NEARLY DONE" (16" x 20") by William Henry Boucher, a German artist who made fascinating domestic and social pictures, choosing his subjects mostly from Dendy Sadler; and "THE HAMLET" (16" x 20"), designed and etched by Dasselborne, a French artist. The first shows two young women putting the finishing stitches in a patchwork quilt; the second a white cottage with mandarin-colored roof, a dark green river, and trees half stripped of leafage, made lovely by the golden haze of autumn. Both pictures are handled with delicate skill. The colors are wonderfully blended. [The current location of these etchings is unknown. Ed.]

LITHOGRAPHY

The art of lithography "owes its success to the mutual antipathy of grease and water" (Slater 43). If a design is put on a porous stone or metal with fatty ink, the stone then moistened, and a roller covered with a greasy or resinous substance pressed over its surface, the design will receive the ink, while the moistened part between will remain clear. In consequence, the design will appear only in the impression or lithographic print that will later be obtained from the stone.

Lithography was discovered in 1796 by a Bavarian printer, Alois Senefelder. From Munich, where Senefelder made his experiments, it spread to other centers in Europe and finally America. Like the other arts of engraving, it has had its ups and downs, at one time meeting with great public acclaim, at another with almost complete forgetfulness. Some thirty or forty years ago it became extinct. But an art the possibilities of which have attracted masters like Whistler, Prout, James Ward, and John Copley is bound to survive, and today many artists are again turning to lithography as an adaptable medium of expression.

Quest of the Holy Grail: Panel I: "The Vision, or The Infancy of Galahad"

"THE HOLY GRAIL"

Abundant wall space in the main corridor of Tower Hall affords a good setting for fifteen lithographic prints made after the mural paintings of the Holy Grail by Edwin Austin Abbey. The originals after which these were done are on the walls of the Boston Public Library, the largest being twenty-eight feet by sixteen feet in size. Our lithographs are one-fourth the size of the paintings. They constitute an impressive series, interesting alike for their beauty and the idealism of their story. [The black and white lithographs were hand-colored by Sister Salome Blais. The panels are too large to photograph. The drawings here are postcard reproductions, courtesy of the Trustees of the Boston Public Library. Ed.]

Abbey took his theme from the Arthurian romances, probably from Malory's Compilation, (*Le Morte d'Arthur*) using only that part of the legends that dealt with the quest of the Sacred Vessel from which our Lord partook at the Last Supper.

An interesting story can be told by grouping the prints into three divisions of five pictures each. Unity is achieved in the entire series by the figure of Galahad clothed in scarlet "like a vivid spirit informing each part" (Malory). [Galahad is often called the Red Knight. A quotation from one of the old stories explains: "And as at Whitsuntide the Holy Spirit came to the Apostles in guise of fire, so at Whitsuntide Galahad came clad in red. It has been suggested that white is the color of untried

The first five, which depict the "Preparation for the Quest," begin with the appearance of the infant Galahad, who has been vouchsafed the "Vision of the Grail." In a mysterious way, he is placed in a convent of white-clad nuns where he is trained in courage, purity, faith, and the other virtues befitting a knight destined for a holy enterprise. The second picture shows him, now a man, taking the "Oath of Knighthood," then going forth accompanied by two other knights to the castle of King Arthur. There he is led by the spirit of his ancestor, Joseph of Arimathea, to the "Siege Perilous." While the King rises to receive him, the Round Table of knights with sword hilts lifted high, foreshadow the conflicts he must encounter in the course of his sacred undertaking.

In the fourth panel, "Benediction upon the Quest," the new leader with many others of the Round Table assemble in the Cathedral to receive the blessing of God on their undertaking. The kneeling knights in armor hold erect their lances, gay with banners of manifold heraldic designs. Galahad kneels in front. His head is bared in reverence, but his left hand grasps a sword, his right a lance. He is ready for the enemies he anticipates meeting in the next episode, which is pictured in "The Castle of the Grail." But this fifth panel suggests a conflict of intellect and spirit, not of swords and lances, for the castle and the shadowy figures within it are under a spell of enchantment. Long have the enchanted ones awaited release; but although the arrival of the pure knight and his followers casts a gleam of light upon the somber place, deliverance is to be purchased only through greater renunciation on the part of the hero. In this, his last conquest over fear and doubt, Galahad's preparation will become complete.

Pictures six to ten inclusive depict the finding of the Sacred Vessel. In the first of these, "The Loathly Damsels," Galahad, who has failed to ask the questions that would have broken the spell, is first seen wandering in a blighted country near the castle. There he meets three maidens, also in confined imprisonment. When they reproach him for his failure, he makes his final act of renunciation; then, strengthened and sustained by Divine Grace, he engages in a terrible fight against seven knights who symbolize the Seven Deadly Sins. Now is the hour of deliverance, for having overcome these evil knights who have barred the way to the castle, Galahad is able to penetrate the interior wall and with uncovered head to receive the "Keys of the Castle" (eighth panel) from an aged keeper, who represents righteousness. The entrance is now clear to the "Castle of the Maidens," depicted in the ninth panel. Being set free, the imprisoned virtues begin to gladden the world with those manifold activities that had been kept enchained by the Seven Deadly Sins. This completes the victory of Galahad over his external foes. His final conquest—complete interior renunciation of self—is seen in the tenth panel, "*Blanchefleur*," in which he renounces

Quest of the Holy Grail: Panel II: "The Oath of Knighthood"

Quest of the Holy Grail: Panel III: "The Round Table of King Arthur (top),
Panel IV: "The Departure" (middle), and Panel V: "The Castle of the Grail" (bottom)

earthly love, breaks with his beautiful bride-elect, and dedicates himself entirely to the completion of his holy vow.

The rewards that are the fruit of spiritual achievement are portrayed in the last five panels, named in order: "Death of Amfortas," "Galahad the Deliverer," "Solomon's Ship," "The City of Sarras," and "The Golden Tree." In the first we see King Amfortas, leader of the knights who had been under the spell of enchantment. Galahad has released the king and his subjects, and Amfortas, dying, is privileged to behold the Grail as an angel bears it away.

The next scene shows Galahad surrounded by a grateful people who hail him as their King-to-be. But still another victory must be won before he can achieve this award; he must make a voyage in Solomon's Ship, a symbol of the wisdom necessary to bear him to complete enlightenment. He enters into the frail bark, which glides safely through the stormy waves until it reaches the City of Sarras, mystically represented in the thirteenth scene as the Land of Promise and the last earthly abode of Galahad. Arrived there he is made King, replacing Amfortas, because he has made himself lord

of his own soul and all else has been given him. He builds the wondrous Golden Tree of the final panel, symbol of his perfected works, and is permitted to see once more the Grail itself and to make the supreme sacrifice: "Now blessed Lord, would I no longer live." Divine Wisdom has been attained.

Although the story of the quest is founded on the apocryphal scripture, it has a religio-cultural significance and a connection with historical places that make it appealing. To cite a single instance: Avalon is now identified with the Monastery of Glastonbury (Sterling 221). The story is likewise imbued with religious idealism. Its mystical quality has appealed to poets of every land and time—Chretien de Troyes, Malory, Milton, Tennyson—to name only a few. Certainly it lends itself to artistic presentation by its colorful pageantry and wealth of dramatic incident. Its appeal in pictorial art has been no less effective. A knowledge of the theme occasions many a tour into our cultural past. In such a journey we encounter old names and places, events of sacred and profane history, the literature of many lands, and the beauty of holiness. [FOR THE CURRENT LOCATION OF THESE LITHOGRAPHS, SEE APPENDIX A. ED.]

Quest of the Holy Grail: Panel VI: "The Loathely Damsel" (top),
Panel VII: "The Conquest of the Seven Deadly Sins" (bottom left), and Panel VIII: "The Key to the Castle" (bottom right)

Quest of the Holy Grail: Panel IX: "The Castle of the Maidens.(top), Panel X: "Galahad Parts from His Bride, Blanchefleur"
(middle), Panel XI: "The Death of Amfortas" (bottom left) and Panel XII: "Galahad the Deliverer" (bottom right)

Quest of the Holy Grail: Panel XIII: "The Voyage to Sarras" (top), Panel XIV: "The City of Sarras" (middle),
and Panel XV: "The Golden Tree, and the Achievement of the Grail" (bottom)

Appendix A

Present Locations of Statues and Art Work

Our Lady of Victory

In storage at St. Mary's Medical Center

Stations of the Cross

Current Chapel ambulatories

St. Benedict and St. Scholastica, wood, early styles

Entrance to the Monastery of St. Scholastica at the end of the east cloister walk

St. Benedict and St. Scholastica, Gothic style

Monastery Dining Room, Stanbrook Hall, first floor

Canopies for these statues:

one in Monastery parlor
one in storage

Our Lady of Grace

Tower Hall, main entrance

St. Thomas More

College Library, third floor

Cardinal Newman

College Library, third floor

Christ the King, wood, contemporary

Tower Hall, first floor

Holy Family (Christmas Creche) wood, contemporary

Chapel gathering space during Christmas season

Crucifix, wood, contemporary

Monastery dining room, Stanbrook Hall, first floor

"The Last Meeting of Saint Benedict and Saint Scholastica"

Tower Hall lobby

"The Assumption"

Monastery Heritage Room, Stanbrook Hall, third floor

"Consummatum Est"

Monastery Community Room, Stanbrook Hall, third floor

"Light in the Darkness"

Monastery Community Room, Stanbrook Hall, third floor

"Light in the Light"

Monastery Community Room, Stanbrook Hall, third floor

"The Madonna and Child"

Stanbrook Hall, second floor

"Saint Agnes"

Stanbrook Hall, third floor

"November Afternoon at Chester Creek"

Stanbrook Hall, first floor

"Winter in Tennessee"

Stanbrook West, third floor

"First Snowfall in Yedo"

Stanbrook West, third floor

"Roman Scenes"

Stanbrook Hall, third floor

"The Holy Grail"

Tower Hall, first floor

Appendix B

Descriptions of Building Renovations

Original Chapel

Bell Tower

The bell tower is in its original space, but the ringing of the bells is now automated.

Narthex

The flooring and woodwork of the original Chapel narthex can be seen in the entrance to The College of St. Scholastica Library.

Holy Water Fonts

The holy water fonts from the original Chapel are in Rockhurst dining room on the first floor of Stanbrook Hall.

Baldachin

Four angels from the original baldachin were transferred to the current Chapel altar, two are mounted at the cloister walk entrance to Stanbrook Hall, and two smaller carvings are on the funeral bier.

Stained Glass Windows

The original leaded windows depicting St. Scholastica, St. Gertrude, and St. Hildegarde are in the Benedicine Devotional Area to the right of the altar. The remainder of the windows are in the Gathering Space of the Chapel. They have been redone without the original leading and colored background. The windows from the clerestory are now in the Eucharistic Chapel.

Original Chapel, *continued …*

Great East Window, Our Lady Queen of Peace

This window can be seen from the second and third floors of the current library.

Metal gates from the altar railing of the original Chapel

The gates were used to make moveable altar tables for the chapel in Benet Hall on the second floor of Stanbrook Hall and Rockhurst Meeting Room on the first floor of Stanbrook Hall.

Altar Crucifix

The corpus from the altar crucifix is in the Eucharistic Chapel.

Rockhurst Auditorium

The auditorium was converted into a dining room and meeting rooms for the Monastery.

Stanbrook Hall

Stanbrook Hall was remodeled to become St. Scholastica Monastery with offices, Benet Hall (assisted living for infirm Sisters), and residences for Sisters.

Appendix C

Donors

Main Altar, Tabernacle, Baldachin:
The Most Reverend Thomas A. Welch, D.D.

Sanctuary Lamps:
Monsignor Patrick Byrnes

Hand-carved Organ Grille:
Monsignor George Gallik

Organ Fund:
Priests of the Diocese

Stations of the Cross:
The Honorable Martin Hughes

Altar Crucifix:
Mr. P. M. O'Meara

Bishop's Cathedra and Priedieu:
Mr. and Mrs. E. B. Hansen

Pulpit and Communion Rail:
Miss Elizabeth Ries

Sanctuary Gates:
Mr. and Mrs. Edward J. Scanlon

Altar and Tabernacle in the Lady Chapel:
Students of The College of St. Scholastica

Altar in St. Joseph Chapel:
Mrs. Margaret Lamb

High Candlesticks on the Main Altar:
Miss Emily Milette

Low Candlesticks on the Main Altar:
Mr. James McCue

Credence Table:
Miss Jean Bertrand

Bookstands in Transept Chapels:
Mr. C.E. Jones

Chapel Bell:
Mr. and Mrs. Patrick Agnew

Great East Window: Our Lady Queen of Peace
The College Alumnae Association 1937-1941

Major Windows of the Ambulatories:

St. Catherine of Alexandria:
A Friend

St. Anne:
Miss Anna Brooks, Alumna of Sacred Heart Institute

St. Elizabeth of Hungary:
Friends of Sister M. Julianna Rosch

Blessed Kateri Tekakwitha:
Students of St. Timothy's School, Chicago

Mother Cabrini:
Friends of Sister M. Immaculate McCauley

St. Therese of the Child Jesus:
Friends of Sister M. DeChantal Blais

St. Cecilia:
Friends of St. Joseph's Hospital, Brainerd

St. Martha:

Mrs. Con O'Brian

St. Agnes:

Miss Mary Laughlin

St. Scholastica:

Miss Mary Kaminska, Alumna of Sacred Heart Institute

St. Gertrude:

Students of Stanbrook Hall

St. Hildegarde:

Student nurses

St. Genevieve:

State College Clubs

St. Catherine of Siena:

Mr. Con O'Brian

St. Brigid of Ireland:

Friends of Sister M. Philip Roche

St. Joan of Arc:

Friends of Sister M. Salome Blais

Windows of Ambulatory Walls:

Miss Elizabeth Ries
Dr. E. L. Tuohy

Windows of Transept Chapels:

Rev. Andrew Gallik
Mrs. Clarence Graham
Miss Katherine McMillan, Alumna of the College
Miss Nell Cavender
Mr. and Mrs. Peter Sauer
Mrs. J. McDonald

Windows of the Clerestory and the Narthex:

All these windows were donated by the non-resident students of the College, by friends of the Sisters, or by casual visitors who, while viewing the new Chapel during its construction, expressed a wish to donate to a chapel that would be dedicated to Our Lady Queen of Peace.

St. Benedict and St. Scholastica (Gothic Style):

Bishop John T. McNicholas, Christmas 1925

Our Lady of Grace:

Blessed Virgin Sodality, 1930

St. Thomas More and Cardinal Newman:

Blessed Virgin Sodality of the College, 1942-1944

Our Lady of Victory:

Right Reverend Patrick Byrnes

"Our Lady of Refuge":

Students of the College, 1937-1940

"St. Joseph":

Friends of Sister M. Roberta Fleckenstein

"Last Meeting of St. Benedict and St. Scholastica":

Alumnae Association, 1929

"The Assumption":

Mrs. Shores Walker, 1938

"St. Agnes":

Bishop James McGolrick

"First Snowfall in Yedo":

Most Reverend Thomas A. Welch

Holy Grail Series:

*Students of the College and Academy
1917-1934*

Appendix D

ARCHITECTS OF CAMPUS BUILDINGS

In 1906 Mother Scholastica hired the Duluth architectural firm of Frederick German and A. Werner Lignell to draw up plans for a building on the Kenwood Avenue site. German and Lignell went on, individually and collectively, to design a number of Duluth residences and commercial buildings. Their plan for Villa Scholastica was delivered in 1906, and the drawing was published in the *Duluth News Tribune* with an article describing the Sisters' new venture.

The building was three stories in a quasi-Tudor style favored by the firm. Note that there is only one tower and that a chapel is located at the far west end of a wing.

The plan was to build in stages, and the first stage was the section south of the tower, and two westward-extending wings at either end. As building progressed during 1907–'08, it was brought to the attention of the Sisters by independent observers that the construction was faulty, and the building was in danger of collapsing. Sister Agnes in another account charitably attributes this to the relative inexperience of the architects and contractor, although later interpretations included the possibility of anti-Catholic feeling.

Mother Scholastica fired both the architects (who according to Sister Agnes "tore up their plans" as they left) and the contractor, and set out to find someone to rescue the partially completed building. She turned to the building inspector for the city of St. Paul, Franklin Ellerbe. Ellerbe came to Duluth, inspected the building, and agreed to rescue it. He prepared his own proposed plan for the completed building, which in the interim had expanded to four stories, but still owed most of its inspiration to the original German and

A 1906 drawing of Villa St. Scholastica based on plans by architects Frederick German and A. Werner Lignell, which called for just three stories

A drawing based on plans for Franklin Ellerbe's four-story design for Villa Scholastica

Lignell plan. The first stage of construction, the south end of the proposed structure was completed in 1909, and the Sisters and students moved in.

Franklin Ellerbe was so encouraged by his success that he decided to make architecture his career and went on to found the nationally-known Ellerbe architectural firm. Together with his son Thomas, he designed a large number of educational and health facility buildings in Minnesota. Interestingly enough, the Ellerbe drawing was included in all of the College publications until the actual construction of the north extension in 1927.

In 1911 Franklin Ellerbe supervised the building of the second west-trending wing, and in 1918-19 his firm, now Ellerbe and Round, planned an addition to the northwest wing, and added a second floor to the garage. Following the original Ellerbe plan, more or less, the first (south) tower was added in 1921-22.

In 1927, under the leadership of Mother Agnes Somers, the architectural firm of O'Meara and Hills from St. Louis was chosen to complete Tower Hall, with the addition of the north tower (in Medieval tradition, in a slightly different style from the south tower) and the north extension. The St. Louis firm also oversaw the interior décor particularly of the lobby and parlors.

The same St. Louis firm, now O'Meara, Hills and Quick, was chosen by Mother Agnes in 1937 for the design of the Chapel/library and Stanbrook Hall. The Chapel was neo-Romanesque, as is fitting for a Benedictine monastery, and Stanbrook, particularly the interiors, shows a strong art deco influence fitting to the period of its construction.

— SISTER MARGARET CLARKE, OSB
MONASTERY ARCHIVIST

Works Cited

Academic Announcement for 1892 – 93. Munger Terrace, Duluth, MN.

Aquinas, St. Thomas. *Summa Theologica.* Chicago: Encyclopedia Britannica, 1952.

Benedict, Saint. *The Rule of St. Benedict.* St. Louis: Herder, 1907.

Burton, E. "Thomas More." *Catholic Encyclopedia.* New York: Appleton, 1907 – 1914.

Catalog of The College of St. Scholastica. 1913 – 1914; 1937 – 1938.

Collins, Harold E. *The Church Edifice and Its Appointments.* Philadelphia: Dolphin, 1940.

Delatte, Paul. *The Rule of St. Benedict: A Commentary.* New York: Benziger, 1921.

Donohue, Harry Eversfield. *Letter to Sister Agnes Somers, OSB.* 13 December 1948.

Duluth Catholic Register. 21 August 1938.

Fargo, Lucille. *The Library and the School.* Chicago: American Library Association, 1947.

Files of the Registrar, The College of St. Scholastica.

Forbes, Frances Alice. *St. Benedict.* London: Burns, 1921.

Gregory I, Pope. *Life and Miracles of St. Benedict.* Trans. Odo J. Zimmerman and Benedict R. Avery. Collegeville, MN: Abbey P, 1949.

Hakel, Toto Yukemi. *Eight Snow Scenes of the Eastern Capitol by Ichiryusai Heroshige.* Kyoto, Japan: Shotaro Sato, 1928.

Institute Echoes, 1.1 (January 1902).

Laws of Minnesota Relating to the Public School System. St. Paul, MN: 1939.

Malory, Thomas. *Le Morte D'Arthur.* New York: Dutton, 1926. Vol. 2 Everyman's Library.

Maritain, Jacques. *Art and Scholasticism, with Other Essays.* Trans. J. F. Scanlan. New York: Scribners, 1947.

Newman, John Henry. *The Idea of a University.* Garden City, NY: Image Books, 1949.

———. "The Mission of St. Benedict." *Historical Sketches, Vol. 2.* London: Longmans, 1899. 365 – 430.

Parsons, E. Dudley. *The Story of Minnesota.* New York: American Books, 1916.

Pius X, Pope. *Motu Proprio.* Toledo, Ohio: Gregorian Institute of America, 1950.

Pius XII, Pope. *Mediator Dei.* New York: America Press, 1948.

Predmore, Gregory. *Sacred Music and the Catholic Church.* Boston: McLaughlin, 1936.

"Scholastica's New Organ to be Dedicated on June 26." *Duluth Catholic Register.* 19 June 1949, 1.

Schuster, Ildephonso. *St. Benedict and His Times.* Trans. Gregory J. Roettger. St. Louis: Herder, 1951.

Slater, John Herbert. *Engravings and Their Value.* 6th ed. London: Bazaar, 1929.

Sterling, Mary Blackwell. *The Story of Sir Galahad.* New York: Dutton, 1908.

Thwaites, Rueben G. *Jesuit Relations and Allied Documents (1610 - 1791).* New York: Boni, 1925.

Van Treeck, Carl, and Aloysius Croft. *Symbols in the Church.* Milwaukee: Bruce, 1936.

Villa Scholastica Catalog. 1900 – 1901; 1912 – 1913.

Villa Scholastica Quarterly. 1911 – 1928.

Works Consulted

Archives of The College of St. Scholastica. 1928 – 1938.

Annals of the Sisters of St. Benedict. 1900 – 1952.

Birmingham, M. Digna, OSB. *First Fifteen Years*. New York: McMullen, 1947.

Bulletin of The College of St. Scholastica. 1912 – 1952.

Busch, William. *Eucharistia*. St. Paul, MN: Lohmann, 1926.

— — —. *The Mass Drama*. Collegeville, MN: Abbey P, 1930.

Butler, Alban. *Lives of the Saints*. New York: Benziger, 1894.

Cabrol, Fernand. *The Roman Missal*. New York: Kennedy, 1921.

Caecilian. Boston: McLaughlin, 1903 – 1956.

Cheyney, Sheldon. *A Story of Modern Art*. New York: Viking, 1941.

— — —. *A World History of Art*. New York: Viking P, 1946.

Clouzet, Henre. V*itroux Moderne L'Illustrarion*. Numere le Noel, 1936.

Cram, Ralph Adams. *The Substance of Gothic*. Boston: Marshall, 1925.

Dictionnaire D'Archeologie et de Liturgie. Tomes 1 – 6. Paris: Letourzey et Ane, 1910 – 1935.

Ellard, Gerald. *Christian Life and Worship*. Milwaukee: Bruce, 1933.

— — —. *Mass of the Future*. Milwaukee: Bruce, 1948.

Frei, Emil. *Letter to Sister Agnes Somers, OSB*. (n.d.).

Howard, M. *A Study in Symbolism*. London: Theosophical Publishing Society, 1916.

Huysmans, Joris-Karl. *The Cathedral: Stained Glass Tours in France*. New York: Dutton, 1920.

Institute Echoes. 1902 – 1909.

Kelly, Blanche Mary. *The Sudden Rose*. New York: Sheed, 1939.

Kimball, Fiske and George Harold Edgell. *A History of Architecture*. New York: Harper, 1918.

Knapp, M. Justina, OSB. *Christian Symbols and How to Use Them*. Milwaukee: Bruce, 1935.

Konody, P. G., et al. *Painting: an Aid to the Fuller Appreciation of Fine Paintings and a Description of the Various Techniques for the Layman, Student and Artist*. New York: Garden City Publishing, 1935.

LaFarge, Henry A. *Lost Treasures of Europe*. New York: Pantheon, 1946.

Lee, K. D. *Art Then and Now*. New York: Appleton, 1949.

Lydon, Patrick J. *Ready Answers in Canon Law*. New York: Benziger, 1937.

Maynard, Theodore. *Too Small a World*. Milwaukee: Bruce, 1945.

Moran, P. *Via Crucis*. New York: Paulist, 1942.

O'Meara, P. M. and J. B. Hills. *Correspondence*, 1937 – 1939.

— — —. *Plans and Specifications of the Chapel of Our Lady Queen of Peace*. Duluth, MN: 1936.

— — —. *Plans and Specifications of Buildings: Chapel-Library, Rockhurst Auditorium, Stanbrook Hall*. Duluth, MN: July, 1936.

Orate Fratres. Vol. 1 – 24. Collegeville, MN: Liturgical Press, 1926 – 1951.

OSB. *Virgin Saints of the Benedictine Order*. London: Catholic Truth Society, 1903.

Phillipps, Lisle March. *The Works of Man*. New York: Philosophical Library, 1951.

Price, C. Matlack. *The Practical Book of Architecture*. Philadelphia: Lippincott, 1916.

The Psalms: New English Translation. New York: Benziger, 1947.

Robb, David M. and J. J. Garrison. *Art in the Western World*. New York: Harper, 1942.

School Catalog. Munger Terrace and Sacred Heart Institute, 1892 – 1909.

Schwartz, George M. "The Geology of the Duluth Metropolitan Area." *University of Minnesota Geological Survey, Bulletin 33*. Minneapolis: University of Minnesota Press, 1949.

Scriptorium. Vol. 2 – 7. 1932 – 1938.

Sherill, Charles Hitchcock. *Stained Glass Tours in Germany, Austria, and the Rhine Lands*. London: Lane, 1927.

Shipley, O. *Hymns of the Church*. London: Burnes Oates, 1894.

Stites, Raymond Somers. *The Arts and Man*. New York: McGraw, 1940.

Sturgis, Russell, et al. *A Dictionary of Architecture and Building*. New York: Macmillan, 1902.

Towers. 1937 – 1938.

Villa Scholastica Quarterly. 1909 – 1930.

Worship. Vol. 26 – 27. Collegeville, MN: Liturgical P, 1951 – 52.

Index

A

Abbey, Edwin Austin 131
"Academics" 20, 26, 27, 29
Academy
    at Munger Terrace 1-3
    at Villa Sancta Scholastica 13, 20, 31
Accreditation 22
Acts of the Congregation
    of the Sacraments 73, 74
Advisory Board 45
Agnew, Mr. and Mrs. Patrick 25, 139
All-American Honors 54
Alpha Chi Room 33
Alpha Psi Omega 34
Alpha Tau Delta 44
Altar(s)
    Chapel 41, 73, 74, 138, 139
    Altar Appointments 73-77
    Side Altars 70, 75
    Crucifix 76, 138, 139
    Vestments, Veils, and Vestment Case 77
Alumnae Association 51, 139, 140
American Association of Collegiate
    Schools of Nursing 35
American Association of University
    Women 48
American College Association 34
American Protective Association
    (A.P.A.) 1
Angel(s) 66, 74, 75, 109, 138
Angelus Court 65, 109
Anthony a Wood 11, 17
Anti-garb law 39, 40
Architectural styles on campus
    American (modern) 62, 63
    Early Christian 73, 74, 75, 76, 106
    English Derivative 58
    English Tudor 58, 59, 60, 141
    Romanesque 60, 64, 67, 69, 73, 75,
        83, 106, 142
Arthur, King 131-133
"Assumption, The" 119, 120, 137
Athletic Association 34

B

Bachelor(s) degrees 24, 28, 29, 40, 42
    Baldachin 69, 70, 74, 75, 138, 139

"Ballet of Ballianalula" 126-127
Barry, Geraldine 26
Bartha, Maria 1, 20
Bear visits the College 46
Bell (and Bell Tower) 25, 65, 66, 138, 139
Benedictine Sisters' Academy
    at Munger Terrace 2, 3
Benedictines 9, 17, 95, 119
Berlinger, Victor 109, 110
Berry, Cecelia Rae 26
Bertrand, Jean 139
Birkholz, Sister Benedict, OSB 113
Birmingham, Sister Digna, OSB 47
Bishops of the Diocese of Duluth
    McGolrick, James 1, 2, 4, 6, 7, 8, 24,
        25, 140
    McNicholas, John T., OP 24, 25, 46,
        107, 140
    Welch, Thomas 27, 28, 41, 139, 140
Blais, Sister Salome, OSB 12, 126, 131
Boardman, Charles 31
Boland, Right Rev. Michael 78
"Book Brigade" 42
Boston Public Library 131
Boucher, William Henry 130
Braegelman, Sister Athanasius, OSB 48
Braun, Sister Joan, OSB .... vi, vii, 82
Brewer, Ralph 125, 126
Brooks, Anna 139
Buecheler, Rev. Louis 115
Burgess, Elizabeth 35
Busch, Rev. William 97
Bush, Sister Mary Scholastica, OSB 49
Business Education 42, 43
Byrnes, Msgr. Patrick 34, 41, 51, 116,
    139, 140

C

Cabrini, Mother 87, 139
Cadet nursing program 35, 45
Cameron, E. H. 32, 33
Campanile 65
Campbell, Sister Yvonne, OSB 77
Cancer research 46, 47
Canon Law 73
Cannon, Sister Florentine, OSB 3

Cannon, Sister Jeremia, OSB 4
Cashen, Rev. Joseph 42
Catholic University 22, 23, 24, 35, 47
Cavender, Nell 140
Chapel
    altar 73, 74
    baldachin 69, 70, 74, 75, 138, 139
    bell and bell tower 25, 65, 66
    campanile 65
    facade 66, 67
    narthex 68
    nave 69
    organ(s) 45, 100-102
    sacristy 69
    sanctuary 69, 70
    tabernacle 74
    transept (side) chapels 70, 75
Chapel in Autumn
    (Sister Salome Blais painting) 12
Chapel in Tower Hall 23, 25
Chapel of Our Lady Queen of Peace .... iv,
    37, 40, 41, 57, 64, 66, 68, 69, 73-82, 83, 96,
    100, 101, 102, 104, 138
Chattersheet, The 44
Chester Creek 14, 20, 21
Chester Park 13, 14
Christ the King
    statue 112, 137
    feast 100, 103
Christmas banquet 25, 28, 43
Christmas creche 112, 137
Clerestory 69, 84, 138, 140
Cloister walk(s) 37, 39, 41, 60, 61, 64, 65,
    105, 106
Coat of Arms, College x
"College Chronicle" 27
College of St. Catherine 24
College of St. Scholastica, The
    Advisory board 45
    Coat of Arms x
    Curriculum 1925-1950 42
    Elevation 8, 13
    Founding 19
    Four-year college 26, 28, 29
    Library 33, 41, 42, 49, 50, 51,
        70, 71, 72, 110, 137
    Location 7, 8, 9-17
    Motto .... ix, x

Social/recreational life........ 20, 21, 30, 32-35, 43-51
Song ("Vivat!") 31
Symbolic customs 36, 37
Junior college................................. 19, 20, 23
"Collegiates" 20, 26, 27
Communion rail 69, 76, 139
Compline 99
Conception Abbey........................... 95, 96, 98
Conservatory of Music 25, 26
Constitutional Provisions of the Public School System of Minnesota 39
"Consummatum Est" 121, 137
Convocation(s) 34, 37
Course of study
Munger Terrace 1892-93......................... 2, 3
Sacred Heart Institute 1900 .... 5, 6
Junior college 1912 20
College expansion years 42, 57
Crago, Mrs. William..51
Crowning of Mary.................... 100, 102, 108
Crucifix 75, 76, 113
Currie, Rev. Myron...42

D

"Daisy Farm" 5, 6, 7, 8
Dasselborne 130
Day Students 4, 48
Dick, A. L...129
Dietetics 42, 43
Diocese (of Duluth).....1, 24, 25, 36, 124, 139
Divine Office 8, 89, 97, 98, 99
Donohue, Harry Eversfield 76, 78
Duluth Catholic Register 41, 101
Duluth
weather 11, 12
geology 9, 10, 11, 15
Duluth gabbro..............................9, 10, 15
Duluth State Teachers' College 39, 40
Dunphy, Sister Pauline, OSB 3

E

Eamon, Father Bernard 98
Echoes, Institute 5, 8
"Egyptian Fair, The" 123
Elementary Education 40, 43
Ellard, Rev. Gerald.....................................97
Ellerbe, Franklin 141
Encyclical on Sacred Music 100
Engraved prints..127
Etching(s) 118, 119, 127, 129, 130, 131

Eucharistic Chapel...............................84, 138

F

Faculty Institute 45
Fairview Heights...13
Falkner, John 126
Farley, James 34
First Fifteen Years 47
"First Snowfall in Yedo" 127, 128, 137, 140
Fleming, Sister Hyacinth, OSB 97
Four-year college 26, 28, 29
Foyer Parlor, Tower Hall...................59, 125
Frei, Emil 94

G

Gabriel, Archangel (stone statue) 109
Galahad...131-135
Gallik, Msgr. George 75, 139
Gallik, Rev. Andrew 140
Gatey, Louis 118
German, Frederick 141
Gertken, Rev. Norbert, OSB.......................98
Gleason, Rev. David 42
Gleason, Sister Basil (Theresa), OSB.........23
Glenn, Lawrence, Rev................................42
Gowan, Sister Olivia, OSB.........................35
Graduate Record Examination 43, 45
Graham, Mrs. Clarence..............................140
Great East Window 66, 83, 84, 93, 94, 138, 139
Gregorian chant.....................95-98, 103-104
Gruetter, Sister Agatha, OSB......................25
Guilfoyle, Rev. William 41
Gymnasium.................17, 22, 26, 57, 58, 101

H

Hakel, Toto Yukemi.................................128
Hamilton, Hamel 129
"Hamlet, The" 130
Hammenstede, Prior 97
"Hanging of the Crane" 129
Hansen, Mr. and Mrs. E. B. 139
Heinzeller, Hans.............................. 112, 113
Heldner, Knute 126
High School Standard
Special Certificate.............................43
Hill, Louis and Maud
Family Foundation..............................47
Hills, J. B. 109
Hilton, Mrs. Afton....................................51

Hiroshige, Ichiryusai................................128
History of Legislation Affecting Private Elementary and Secondary Schools.........47
"Holy Grail, The" 131-137, 140
Holy water fonts.............................69, 138
Home Economics 33, 42, 43
Honors Examinations 43
Huegle, Dom Gregory, OSB 96
Hughes, Judge Martin 51, 139
Hughes, Sister Martina, OSB 97

I

Idea of a University 11
"Immaculate Conception" statue..............106
Institute Echoes.......................................5, 8
Institutum Divi Thomae 46

J

Jesuit Explorers 13
Jesuit Relations, The 51
Jones, C. E. 139
Jones, Francis 129
Joseph of Arimethea...................... 81, 132

K

Kakonyi, Sister Constantina......113, 121-123
Kaminska, Mary 140
Kappa Gamma Pi..34
Kerst, Mr. and Mrs. Peter 4
Kerst, Mother Scholastica, OSB..... xii, 1, 3, 8
Kerst, Sister Alexia, OSB...........................19

L

Lady Chapel..75, 77
"Lady Templeton and Son"........................129
Lake Superior 8, 13, 126
Lamb, Alice 51
Lamb, Sister Alice, OSB 113
Lamb, Mrs. Margaret 139
Landscape Paintings.................................125
"Last Meeting of Saint Benedict and Saint Scholastica, The"............118, 119, 137, 140
"Last Supper, The" 129
Laughlin, Mary 140
Lawrence, Rev. Emeric, OSB......................98
Lefevre, Rev. Francois 98
Leithner, Sister Augustine, OSB 4
Lenta, Sister Petra, OSB 46
Library....................31, 33, 37, 42, 49, 50, 51, 70-72, 142
"Light in the Darkness"............121-122, 137

"Light in the Light" 122, 137
Lignell, A. Werner 141
Line Engraving 127, 129
Lithography 131
Liturgical practices in the
    parish schools 102-105
Liturgical Revival .... ix, 95-101

M
Madea, Yujiro 128
"Madonna of Trust, The" 123
Maguolo, Mr. 105
Malory 131, 134
Maryglade 15, 16, 33, 34, 46, 115
Materials used in campus buildings
    Blue trap granite 58, 59, 60
    Florentine glass 59
    Genevieve Rose marble 69
    Limestone (Indiana, Bedford,
        or white) 59, 61, 62, 66, 109, 110
    Kesota/Winona marble
        (Oneota Dolomite) 59, 73, 75
    Morocco Red marble 69
    Nemadji tile 59
    Paneling, wormy chestnut 59
    Parget ceiling 59
    St. Cloud granite 60-62
McCarthy, Sister Katharine, OSB 4, 20,
    22, 50
McCue, James 139
McDonald, Mrs. J. 140
McGolrick, Bishop James 1, 2, 4, 7, 8,
    24, 25, 140
McLaughlin, Sister Raymond, OSB 47
McMillan, Katherine 140
McNicholas, Bishop John T., O.P. 24, 25,
    28, 46, 140
Medical Record Librarian 42
Medical Technology 42
Mezzotint 129, 130
Michigan Club 37
Milette, Emily 139
Minnesota College Association 34
Minnesota (State) Department of
    Education 23, 43
(Minnesota) Department of Public
    Instruction 29
Missa Cantata 104
Missa Recitata 92, 98, 103
Monte Cassino 9, 120, 130
Moquereau, Dom Andre, OSB 96, 97

More, Dame Gertrude 37
Motto (College) ....ix, x
Munger Terrace 1, 2, 3, 4

N
Narthex 68, 69, 70, 84, 93, 138, 140
Nave 41, 68, 69
"Nearly Done" 130
Newman, John Henry, Cardinal 11, 17,
    111, 137, 140
Nieuvencamp, W. O. J. 127
Nine Ideals 36, 37, 54
Normal School at CSS 23, 39
North Central Association 31, 32, 33,
    44, 48
Notker, Brother 129, 130
"November Afternoon at
    Chester Creek" 125, 126, 137
Nursing Education 42

O
O'Brian, Mr. and Mrs. Con 140
O'Donnell, Sister Rose, OSB 48
Oil Paintings 117
"Old Bridge" 127, 128
O'Meara, Hills, and Quick 37, 142
O'Meara, P.M. 139
Opus Dei 89, 99
Ora et Labora (motto) 118,119
"Ora et Labora" (mural) 119, 120
Orate Fratres 97
Organ(s)
    Cassavant pipe 45, 101
    Two-manual Kilgen 101
"Our Lady of Grace" 108, 137, 140
"Our Lady of Refuge" 117, 118, 140
Our Lady of Victory
    Shrine 115, 116
    Statue 72, 137, 140
Our Lady Queen of Peace Chapel .... iv,
    37, 40, 41, 64, 66, 67, 68, 73, 74, 75, 83,
    100, 101, 102, 104, 110, 138

P
Parsons, E. Dudley 11
Peik, Dean 47
"Peonies" 126
Phillips, Mr. 32, 36
Physical education 26, 32, 43
Pieta 113, 114

Pius X School of Sacred Music 97
Pope Benedict XV 93
Pope Gregory the Great 118
Pope Pius X 95, 97, 99, 100
Pope Pius XI 34, 93, 100
Post Office 34, 35
Pulpit 76, 77, 139

Q
Queen of the Lake, stone statue 110
Questionnaire Results 1942 .... 24, 47, 48
Questionnaire 1951 47
Questionnaire on Liturgical
    Practices 102, 103, 104
Quick, Berni 120

R
Recreation at the College 20, 30, 34,
    48, 51, 60
Riehl, Sister Agatha, OSB 46
Ries, Elizabeth 140
Rockhurst Auditorium 37, 38, 57, 61,
    63, 138
"Roman Scenes" 130, 137
Rule of St. Benedict 89

S
Sacred Heart Institute 4, 5, 6, 7, 34, 95, 97
Sacred Heart School 40
Sacred Heart shrine 9, 114, 115
Sacred Heart 30" statue 106
Sacristy 69, 77
"Saint Agnes" 123, 124, 137
"Saint Joseph" 118
Sanctuary/Sanctuary
    Appointments 65, 69, 76, 77, 84
"Sand Dunes" 126
Sarazin, Frances 28
Sartain, William 129
Sauber, Sister Leonissa, OSB 3
Sauer, Mr. and Mrs. Peter 140
Scanlon, Mr. and Mrs. Edward 139
Schiller, Gottfried 117, 118
Schoenfel, Susan 119
Schola 98, 104
Scholastican Ideal(s) 36, 37, 54
Schwitalla, Rev. Alphonse 32, 33
Scriptorium 34, 52, 53, 54
Second Look, A 47
Senefelder, Alois 131

Shamrock Lodge 34, 35
Shrines on Campus 113-116
Sholar, Rev. John 51
Shores, Eugene A. 119
Shotaro Sato 128
Shumway, Mr. 31, 32, 33
Side altars..75
Singenberger, John 95, 97
Skating house 37, 45
Slater, Herbert 127
Smith-Hughes Act...43
Smythe, Richard............................. 129, 130
Sodality of the Blessed Mother 45, 53,
     100, 108, 110, 140
Solon, Eleanor 28
Somers, Sister Agnes, OSB ....iv, vii,
     viii, ix, 20, 22, 35, 46, 52, 53, 54, 82, 84,
     121, 142
Spirit 53
St. Agatha..74
St. Agnes..89, 140
St. Agnes Honor Society 34
St. Anne..85, 139
St. Ann's Home for the Aged 4
St. Benedict..9, 59
     (see also St. Scholastica and St. Benedict:
          pairs of statues)
St. Benedict's Academy 1
St. Benedict's Hospital.............................115
St. Brigid of Ireland 92, 140
St. Catherine of Alexandria................85, 130
St. Catherine of Siena....................92, 140
St. Cecilia 88, 139
St. Elizabeth of Hungary.....................86, 139
St. Francis Xavier 93
St. Genevieve.......................................91, 140
St. Gertrude........................... 90, 138, 140
St. Gertrude's School of Arts and Crafts......104
St. Hildegarde.......................... 90, 138, 140
St. Isaac Jogues 93
St. Jean Baptiste Parish Club 34
St. Joan of Arc......................................93, 140
St. John's Abbey..................... 95, 97, 98
St. Joseph Chapel 75, 118, 139
St. Joseph of the Lily, statue...................106
St. Martha 88, 140
St. Mary's Hall....................................34, 45
St. Mary's Hospital.........32, 34, 35, 57, 58, 72
St. Mary's School of Nursing......................34

St. Meinrad's Abbey......................................95
St. Patrick............................... 92, 93, 98
St. Peter Claver...98
St. Rose of Lima..91
St. Scholastica (stained glass)..............89, 140
St. Scholastica, statue 18, 55
St. Scholastica and St. Benedict statues 66,
     105-108, 118-120, 121-122, 137, 140
St. Therese of the Child Jesus 87, 139
St. Thomas Aquinas.....................................71
St. Thomas More...................... 110, 111, 140
St. Thomas School 4
St. Timothy's School 139
St. Vincent 74
Stained glass windows
     Blessed Kateri Tekakwitha 86, 139
     Great East Window..................66, 83, 84, 93,
          94, 138, 139
     Mother Cabrini 87, 139
     St. Agnes..89, 140
     St. Anne 85, 139
     St. Brigid of Ireland............................92, 140
     St. Catherine of Alexandria 85, 139
     St. Catherine of Siena 92, 140
     St. Cecilia 88, 139
     St. Elizabeth of Hungary 86, 139
     St. Genevieve 91, 140
     St. Gertrude 90, 140
     St. Hildegarde 90, 140
     St. Joan of Arc.....................................93, 140
     St. Martha 88, 140
     St. Rose of Lima 91
     St. Scholastica 89, 140
     St. Therese of the Child Jesus 87, 139
Stanbrook Abbey 37
Stanbrook Hall .... iv, 38, 39, 41, 57, 60,
     62, 63, 64, 98, 101, 104, 142
Standardization...31
Stations of the Cross............. 78-82, 137, 139
Statues in Marble, Stone,
     Ceramic 108-111
Statues in Wood
     (Contemporary Styles) 112-113
Statues in Wood (Early Styles)..........105-107
Stewart, Isabel M. 35
Stierlen, Margaret 110
Student Council..34
Sullivan, Sister Celestine, OSB.....................4
"Summer by the Lake" 126
Symbol(s) (ism) ....ix, 25, 36, 59, 62, 69,
     72, 74, 94

T
Tabernacle 74, 75, 139
Tallyho 5, 7
Teachers' College, Duluth..................39, 40
Teachers' College, Superior, WI...............40
Teaching, practice.................... 23, 29, 39, 40
Tekakwitha, Blessed Kateri................86, 139
Thibadeau, Sister Patricia, OSB 43
Three Lakes...34, 35
Touhy, Dr. E.L. 51
Tower Hall ....iv, 17, 23,
     28, 29, 42, 51, 57, 58, 59, 60, 65, 66, 98, 99,
     101, 104, 125, 137, 142
Towers... 37, 52, 54
Transept chapels 70, 84
Trees on campus 15-17
Truman, Rev. Patrick Joseph, OSB.............41

U
University of Minnesota 4, 23, 24, 29,
     31, 33, 47

V
Valley of Silence 14
Vespers 99
Vestment case...69, 77
Victory Hall............................... 45, 57, 72
Villa Sancta Scholastica .... xi, 17, 19, 20,
     22, 26, 27, 56
Villa Scholastica Quarterly................8, 20, 25,
     27, 30
"Visit of the Magi, The"............................120
Vivat! Vivat! St. Scholastica........................31

W
Walker, Mrs. Shores.......................... 119, 140
Ward singing 97
Ward, Mrs. Justine 97, 104
Water color paintings....................... 117, 126
Weaving of the Standards 36
Welch, Bishop Thomas.......27, 28, 41, 51, 74,
     101, 128, 139, 140
"Welcome Visitor, A".................................129
"Winter in Tennessee".................. 126, 137
Wisconsin State Normal School 29
Wood, Anthony a 11, 17
Wood Engraving/Woodcuts.............127-129
World War I..23
World War II 35, 43, 44, 130